# TO MARRY AGAIN

# TO MARRY AGAIN

### by Joel D. Block, Ph.D.

Publishers • GROSSET & DUNLAP • New York
A FILMWAYS COMPANY

*To my parents, Abraham and Rose Block*

The publishers gratefully acknowledge permission to use material from the following:

From *The Divorce Experience* by Morton Hunt and Bernice Hunt. Copyright © 1977 by Morton Hunt and Bernice Hunt. Used with permission of McGraw-Hill Book Company.

From "Stepping In" by Paul Bohannon and Rosemary Erickson. Reprinted from *Psychology Today Magazine,* January, 1978. Copyright © 1977 Ziff-Davis Publishing Co.

From *The Half-Parent: Living with Other People's Children* by Brenda Maddox. Copyright © 1975 by Brenda Maddox. Reprinted by permission of the publisher, M. Evans and Company, Inc., New York, New York 10017.

Adapted from *Marital Separation* by Robert S. Weiss, pp. 236, 241-246. © 1975 by Basic Books, Inc., Publishers, New York.

*Design by Joyce Schnaufer*

Copyright © 1979 by Joel Block
All rights reserved
Published simultaneously in Canada
Library of Congress catalog card number: 78-60461
First printing 1979
ISBN: 0-448-16420-5
Printed in the United States of America

# Contents

| | |
|---|---|
| Introduction | 1 |
| Author's Note | 4 |
| 1. Starting Over | 5 |
| 2. Between Marriages | 13 |
| 3. Previous Attachments: Terminable and Interminable | 32 |
| 4. A New Commitment: Preparing for Remarriage | 52 |
| 5. The Making of a Stepchild | 73 |
| 6. The Impact of "Instant" Children on Marriage | 96 |
| 7. Stepparenting | 114 |
| 8. Keeping the Marital Relationship Strong | 131 |
| 9. Getting There with Help: Marital and Family Therapy | 154 |
| Epilogue | 175 |
| Bibliography | 181 |
| Acknowledgments | 182 |
| Index | 183 |

# Introduction

When I was not quite five, my father died. He died suddenly; there was no time for my mother to prepare herself for the loss. Along with grief she bore many other burdens, including unshared decisions and pressures to accept additional roles. Instantly she had not only to take complete responsibility for children—for my sister and me—but for financial records, transactions, and expenditures that my father had previously managed. A few years later, having struggled with her loss and with the pain muted, my mother married again—and again. I became a stepchild twice. Both marriages—one of seven years' duration and one of three—were terminated by divorce.

All of us—children and adults alike—became, by these events, part of a growing and neglected group in our society—the "blended" or "reconstituted" family. The divorce rate, rising by approximately 8 percent each year, has resulted in an increase in the number of remarriages. In addition, the proportion of remarriages involving children under the age of eighteen has also risen sharply. Although the statistics are incomplete, it is estimated that there are over eight million "reconstituted" families in our society today. Remarriage affects not only the remarried couple but also their children, parents and in-laws, former spouses, friends, and society as a whole. Yet, in contrast to the attention given to nuclear families produced by first marriages, the complexities of subsequent marriages remain all but ignored. Despite social scientists' interest in new trends, very little information has been provided to assist people through the intricacies of remarriage.

In the past, although remarriage was encouraged between the widowed, our culture rejected remarried couples if one or both partners had been divorced. Clergymen were reluctant to perform remarriage ceremonies; laws intended to discourage such unions were passed. Today, although attitudes toward remarriage are changing, remarried people, particularly those with children, are offered no guidelines for coping. If the remarried are no longer viewed with suspicion and disapproval, neither are they assisted in their journey.

Developing new relationships, maintaining a workable one with a former spouse, and providing a nurturant atmosphere for children who become instant steprelations can be quite problematic. There seems to be little realization that when people change marital partners the consequent reorganization is unique and requires a new outlook if it is to be successful. Difficulties arise partly because we do not know how to act toward the remarried and their families, and partly because they are not quite sure what is required of them.

There have been endless articles and books on divorce and a sprinkling on stepparenting. A book that offers guidance for both a new marital relationship and successful stepparenting—a preparatory manual for remarriage and a handbook for making the decision work—seems to be nonexistent. As a psychologist and marital therapist whose own life was touched by this issue, I hope that this book will partly fill the gap.

Every significant emotion and deed described here is drawn from real life. Some of the people have been in therapy with me;

## Introduction

many have not. Although those I talked with do not compose a scientifically chosen sample, neither were they superficially interrogated via the questionnaires of professional pollsters. On the contrary, hours of in-depth, face-to-face discussions, with the assurance of anonymity, provided the very personal reports contained in these pages.

The wisdom, failings, and rich experiences of the remarried are combined with the available scientific research and a decade of clinical practice to describe the perplexities and to suggest guidelines for developing a new love relationship. Nonetheless, no pat answers, no ready-made formulas are prescribed, for in something as complex as remarriage, there are no easy solutions. We humans are decidedly complex; rarely do our lives conform to simple black and white. There are intensities of problems and degrees of solution; some may require therapeutic aid, consequently, suggestions to this effect are periodically offered. Above all, my intent has been to produce an honest guide to the consequences—the dilemmas, traps, and emotional joys—generated by the process of remarriage.

## Author's Note

The identities of the people described herein were protected by altering names and various other external characteristics; the essential psychological and social dynamics involved have been preserved. Any resemblance to real persons is strictly intentional; any identification with particular persons is, I trust, impossible.

# 1 Starting Over

## Highlights

A couple about to take their wedding vows usually approach this very special event with optimism. Inflamed by passion, they marry in hope that their fantasies will spring to life. The wedding day is a sacred occasion, it is the time when a promise is exchanged to love and to cherish and a lifetime partnership is formally announced.

This is the beginning. Some years—or perhaps months—later, the wedding vows have been soiled, the passion and love have been transformed into mutual avoidance, confusion, and unbridled resentment. Each spouse in such a marriage is likely to blame the other for the disappointments and inadequacies that have unraveled the fabric of their union. This is common. It is also common for marriages such as this to end in divorce. This fact, well known by now, is confirmed year after year as the divorce rate soars.

But the facts we have at hand do not warrant publishing the funeral notice of marriage. More people are marrying now than ever before; even the high divorce rate, still growing toward an unknown limit—some counties in this nation have divorce rates as high as 70 percent—does not act as a discouragement; nearly six-sevenths of the divorced remarry. Divorce, for most, is not a sign of disaffection with marriage as an institution but only with an unsuitable partner. Despite the grim effects of divorce, a dream soon forms of a new life, a new partner: "There must be someone out there who understands me, who knows what I really am, and what I really could be."

Michael Wilson has had such a dream. A resident of a small Midwestern suburb, Wilson is unique, as is every person, yet he is much like other people in seeking to reduce the impersonality and disconnected nature of his life. As many do, he has chosen marriage as his antidote. Shy and inhibited in his teens, he had few sexual experiences and no real romances until his senior year in high school; then he met Ginny, fell in love with her, and thereafter never went near another girl. He and Ginny were married in their late teens, while he was in the army.

Wilson, now thirty-six, looks placid, well fed, and uncomplicated; he is husky and of medium height, dresses well but conservatively, has ruffled curly blond hair, a square open face, and the thick, bold features of his farmer ancestors. Michael and Ginny—now thirty-four, a bouncy woman with a short boyish hair style that emphasizes her sprightly features and contrasts with her slightly plump, very curvy body—are divorced. Four years have passed since this painful event. Michael has struggled with his wounds and is currently involved in the process of remarriage.

"The first time I married, I was too young. I had just been drafted and we decided to drive up to Virginia and get married right after my induction. The whole situation was more comic than real—a film in which the action was happening to other people. Neither of us knew what the world was about; we were oblivious to the emotional responsibilities of marriage. Ginny was running away from a mother who was alcoholic; I was over-eager to grow up—to be a man. Marriage, to me, was an almost automatic act, the thing I was supposed to do as part of the 'rites of passage.' "

During the time Michael was in the service and for several years following his discharge, the Wilsons had a marriage of convenience. It was comfortable but not companionable. Although they had passed into adulthood together and were good friends, their interests, goals, and life views had grown unalterably divergent. They had moved to New York where Michael worked with tenacity and single-mindedness to put himself through college; he earned a degree in economics in four years while holding down a full-time job. Working by day in a brokerage firm, going to school at night and all summer, Michael lived on four hours of sleep for weeks at a time. After he got his bachelor's degree, he took further course work and earned a master's degree in business administration. By then he was very successful in the stock market. He was on top—except in his marriage. Ginny was absorbed in her home, their two children—twin girls—and was not interested in any of Michael's activities. He had a similar disinterest, or perhaps even distaste, for Ginny's domestic posture. Theirs was a fragile bond that eventually crumbled. The divorce came after thirteen years of marriage.

"Ginny had custody of the girls and stayed in our home. I rented a small apartment. The first few weeks after our separation were hell. I didn't want to go out. I was depressed, guilty, angry. The flood of emotions overwhelmed me. Then I didn't want to go back to the apartment—it was like having hot and cold chills; first I didn't want to go out and then I would do anything to avoid going back to the apartment. I would go to lousy movies, sit in a bar all night, although I don't like to drink much or talk to dull strangers. Anything to avoid the solitude. At home, I used to work almost every night and come out to have a cup of coffee with Ginny or read to the kids before they went to bed. My work was suffering because I couldn't get those night hours in.

"After the first year I was dating much more. I was pleased with the opportunity to date a variety of women and have diverse sexual experiences. I would go to the bars, clubs, cocktail parties, and all the social gatherings of the 'swinging singles.' This satisfied me for a while, but after a time I wanted a longer-lasting, more meaningful relationship. The stereotype image of the carefree single life did not hold up for me."

Having gone through the agony of marital breakup and the arduous labor of adjustment to postmarital life, Michael found himself moving from emotional isolation, step by step, in ever-closer relationships. Slowly the desire to remarry began to assert itself. Michael continues:

"Once I became more receptive, it wasn't long before I met Joyce. She was divorced with two children. We were very attracted to each other but when, after seven or eight months, we spoke of marriage, both of us were terrified. Two adults, in the prime of life, free to marry, and we were frightened to death! Of what? The children—hers and mine; our former mates; committing ourselves; becoming two-time losers. Things were so much more complicated this time. . . . The children were the biggest complicating factor. They continually involved us in situations that provoked tension and guilt feelings. Once when we were shopping for shoes, the salesman said, 'Now let your daddy see how those fit.' With a disgusted look directed toward Joyce, my new stepson said. '*That* is not my father!' Another time when I tried to get closer, he shouted angrily, 'You don't understand me—you haven't known me all my life!' "

There were also difficulties with Michael's children. He had arranged with Ginny in a series of delicate and painful encounters, to have them spend most weekends with him and Joyce. From Friday evening to Sunday evening, he would play the perfect father, assuaging his guilt for having left them by giving them undivided love and attention. During these times, Joyce was mere background; he hardly seemed aware of her when he had the kids, and he wasn't interested in bringing her into things, or having any kind of normal weekend social life. Whenever Joyce complained, Michael grew tense and felt that she was competing with his children and trying to come between him and them. They had several arguments about this and then Joyce stopped fighting because she saw it was useless; she couldn't get through to him. Joyce spoke to no one about this issue; she was ashamed to. Michael concludes:

"We were both timid about disciplining the other's children, wanting above all to be liked by them. We tried to be understanding and helpful; all the children had been hurt by the divorce and confused by the new alliance. They perceived the divorce as an abandonment by one parent, now they found themselves in the position of being an appendage to a new marriage. As if all this weren't enough, the children provided a permanent link to our ex-spouses, who had their own very strong emotional reactions to our marriage. . . . Despite our previous ambivalence and fear, and considering the emotional booby trap that we are struggling with, Joyce and I are secure in our efforts. There are plenty of unresolved issues, but we feel we have chosen well, certainly better than the first time. This marriage is based on realities rather than on fantasies, on reassuring compatibility rather than on titillating dissimilarity."

Michael Wilson's experience highlights some facets of remarriage. In addition to the burning issues of a first marriage—love, sex, compatibility, and making a living—there are nuances of emotion, coping strategies, and attitudes unique to a second (or third) marriage. Volatile issues erupt out of a terminated marriage about to be reconstituted into a new union. Stepchildren, ex-mates, painful memories, and an extensive network of unfamiliar relationships represent a sizable burden to even the most determined and optimistic among us.

Many people considering remarriage think they know what awaits them. Most are cautious in evaluating the implications of another commitment and are likely to be wiser than they were the first time, yet living with the obligations and demands of remarriage may be more trying than they were able to predict. A good deal of emotional strength is required to orchestrate intrusive relatives, shortage of money, new types of situations, feelings of hate—coming from several directions—and much more.

Even after they have become committed to each other, many people who have been married before are plagued by caution. From their past experience they know that many possibilities exist for disagreement, that love can fade, that their individual lifestyles will be uncovered for close scrutiny, that sensitive differences must be confronted and resolved. Any one of a myriad of difficulties may shake their confidence that remarriage will work. Perhaps he seemed generous at first but later becomes conservative; he gives her a reasonable "table allowance" every week, but she resents having to ask and sometimes being refused, although there is always a reasonable explanation, when she needs "extras" for the children or herself. She believes he ought to do better than he does. He and she may argue about it for hours.

Or perhaps she, who initially appeared independent and self-sufficient, with the bond of remarriage sealed, becomes annoyingly dependent and childlike. After a series of discussions and angry exchanges, they hope the issue is resolved. It may happen that he, who at first liked her children, later becomes jealous of them and sees them as irritants. She, seeing him as impatient and harsh, may in turn feel resentment. This, too, may be confronted but the nagging doubt—a vestige of prior experience—remains: Have we solved the problem or only postponed an issue that will undermine, in subtle increments, the bond between us?

The course of man–woman relationships, even under the best of conditions, has never been known to run smoothly. In remarriage, the path is particularly bumpy. Unlike the young, who commence a relationship relatively unburdened, the formerly married begin their relationship loaded with a great deal of life's baggage. Still, despite all the obstacles and misgivings, the great majority of the previously wed remain the marrying type: Each year over a million men and women meet each other and remarry; at every age level they are more likely to marry than people who have always been single.

Why do the divorced, the widowed, those who have suffered and who know the difficulties of marriage so well, want to remarry? Pressures—exerted by family, friends, children, and society—can be overwhelming. In our coupled world, estrangement from married friends, alienation from many social activities, and an isolated position in the community kindles the temptation to remarry. Add the desire for stability that marriage is supposed to bring, the yearning for someone to share one's social life, the difficulty of living alone and being a lone parent—and the motivation to remarry increases.

Behind the hopeful query posed by well-meaning friends and relatives, "What's new?" looms a more menacing one: "Have you met anybody nice yet; have you found emotional fulfillment yet?" At first the subliminal effect of this message goes unnoticed. However, as time passes, the question wears the formerly married down. If the response is negative, there is a growing feeling of somehow being at fault—"If I am really attractive and desirable, why am I not coupled?" Reinforcing this feeling that "I'm not okay" is the fact that virtually every facet of adult leisure life is dominated by pairs. Not too many of us feel comfortable attending the theater, a restaurant, or a movie alone after years of being part of a pair. We feel conspicuous and ill at ease. In suburbia, the feeling intensifies—the unmarried are aliens who do not belong.

Children also play a large part in transforming a parent into one of the remarried. In a variety of ways, they work at persuading a parent to make a commitment to someone they can envision as a stepparent. Playing on their parent's guilty awareness that they are an incomplete family, they too ask questions —their probes being more transparent than those of adults: "Do you like him/her? Do you think you might marry him/her?" Such veiled pleas can, over a period of time, substantially increase a parent's desire to remarry.

Of course, behind all the motives for remarrying—financial support, security, an additional parent for a child, and reduction of social awkwardness—lies the reason seen as the most noble of all: love. Love is viewed by most of us as the *sine qua non* of life. And marriage is seen as the ultimate expression of an enduring love. Emotional deprivation experienced at the termination of a first marriage makes a loving relationship seem more to be cherished and sought after than ever before. Whatever our age, the desire for a loving relationship continues to burn strongly in practically all of us.

It is no accident that with one love dissolved, this desire for a trustworthy replacement slowly edges toward the center of our being. And it is neither hopeless nor childish fantasy, neither romantic foolishness nor neurotic overdependence, to acknowledge the desire to reach out and love again, to remarry. It is a healthy aspiration; the development of an enduring relationship provides a degree of emotional fulfillment not afforded by other options in life. In a world so impersonal, so disconnected, so unconcerned about the individual's needs, a loving partner provides a large part of what we hunger for.

For those seeking love and commitment in a first marriage, the guidelines for success are plentiful, if not always reliable. Articles on how to enrich marriages can be found in almost every issue of family magazines and weekend newspapers. Similarly, books on marriage abound. People who are considering a second (or third) marriage, however, form a special group, with dramatically different problems. They are pioneers who have to break new ground, largely unaided, without tradition and signposts to show them the way.

The purpose of this book is to help clear the path, to assist those who are or who wish to become involved in a second-chance family—the remarried, their children, stepchildren, and former mates—to help them understand the process, cope with the drawbacks, and realize the very substantial benefits.

# Between Marriages 2

## Unfinished Business

In direct opposition to the forces pulling the formerly married to the promise of rewedded bliss—societal pressure, a desire for companionship, security, and love—are those impeding the way. Nearly all those who have formed a marital bond have shared countless intimacies. The relationship may have been stormy and painful, but there was also caring. For the widowed, the problems of loneliness, practical difficulties, and pressures to remarry are compounded by agonizing memories. Loyalty to a dead mate may form an emotional armor that refuses penetration, for to allow closeness seems an act of betrayal. Betty Mitford is a widow whose experience fits this characterization. She still wears her wedding ring and lives in the same apartment as when she was married. She has kept most of her husband's possessions. Although she is not proud of it, she makes it known that she is a widow to distinguish herself from the divorcées. Betty is forty-seven, her husband has been dead for four years. Physically, she might be described as a "motherly type."

Betty does not talk easily to "strangers." Several of the men she has dated—at the persistent urging of her family—issue a similar report: "Her eyes look through you rather than at you. Not only is the person who lives behind those eyes inaccessible, she doesn't even try to relate. You get the impression she is waiting for you to prove something, or trying to spot a flaw, or sizing you up and finding you wanting."

Undoubtedly, there are a number of widows and widowers who after a period of emotional mourning are able to court a new intimacy. Unfortunately, Betty is not among them; she is having a very difficult time facing life. She has shared her feelings about her husband's death with no one. Four years after his passsing she continues to take tranquilizers in order to sleep. Her attempt to make a life for herself consists of a renewed closeness with her two married daughters. They, in turn, think of her as a responsibility that must be dutifully attended to.

While the widowed and divorced share certain problems, psychologically there are dissimilarities. When a marriage is broken not by fate but by one's own hand, the obstacles to healing are altered. For the divorced, the dissolution of the marriage brings to bear on both husband and wife a complex and confusing interplay of emotions: anger, guilt, sadness, fear, relief, excitement. It is becoming increasingly clear as the numbers of remarried grow that although the final decree promises a release from the bickering, delays, recriminations, legalities, and lawyers, emotions die slowly.

During the period between the initial separation and the completion of the divorce, an emotional digestion process begins. It is the first and most critical step in reorganizing one's life.

Janet Richards is an attractive woman who presents herself as a sort of flower child, yet she is very much in touch with reality. As a former dancer, she retains a beautiful, fluid way of moving. During the majority of the twelve years she was married to Jon —a songwriter and folksinger of moderate success—she thought they had a good marriage. They had good sex, enjoyed each other's company, and felt engaged in a common cause. They had three children. As Jon Richards had become increasingly successful, Janet felt he had become more distant and removed, that he gave her objects and money but not love. She felt relegated to the home and the PTA. Jon felt that his wife was envious of his achievements and had taken on as her personal mission the job of cutting him down to size, that she did not appreciate his accomplishments and wanted to turn the clock back to when they were poor and worked closely together.

Mrs. Richards believed that the man she had loved and married had become materialistic, unloving, ungiving, and essentially hostile to her and probably all women. Her husband felt that *he* was not appreciated or loved, that his wife constantly looked for opportunities to put him down publicly and privately, and that she was therefore probably hostile to all men. They each had their theories regarding the other's problems. Neither could support the other anymore and neither cared to communicate. Each wanted love but insisted the other must be the first to change. For months they traded charges and countercharges. The marriage deteriorated seriously and they arrived at a mutual decision to divorce. In Janet Richards' words:

"The problems of starting over were unanticipated and enormous. Returning to the job market after a ten-year absence was extremely difficult but I did not have the luxury of choice—working was a necessity due to the increased expenses of a split household. I was thrown by the attitude people had toward me as a woman alone. So-called friends dropped me socially. It was as if they thought it was not safe for me to be in·the vicinity of their husbands. I realize that divorce is increasing, but is it also contagious? The loneliness was horrid; hours on the phone or sitting in front of the television were a poor substitute for a mate. I had to learn how to handle money; this was another troubling issue, particularly since my husband and before that my father had always managed the finances. My long-time social and economic dependence left me feeling bereft. I panicked, not occasionally, but frequently. The children became at once a burden, a weapon against Jon, and an incentive to conquer my pain."

The children and money were the two binding agents that

forced Janet and Jon Richards to continue seeing each other. These meetings were sometimes confrontive and always very delicate and painful. As Jon was to reflect, "When a man and woman have lived together for many years, the vestiges of emotional attachment do not dissolve easily." A tone of voice, a gesture, a certain comment—seemingly innocent to an outsider, but filled with special meaning to the former lovers—can suddenly provoke immediate and dramatic anguish. Mrs. Richards continues:

"The resentment between Jon and me ran deep. It was almost two years before we were able to treat each other casually and interact with less intensity. For me, the process was filled with self-pity and hate. When I learned of his plans to remarry, I was crushed. It was like the final rejection. The thought of him with her drove me wild. All that we had worked for—he was making a good living; we had grown up together; I had sacrificed, he had sacrificed—now someone else, rather than I, was savoring the rewards of those difficult years. I couldn't accept the injustice! The fact that our divorce was a mutual decision was no consolation. I was consumed with getting back. I considered jumping into another marriage myself—to show him I was also desirable. I thought of interfering with his marriage—obscene phone calls, exposing his wife to nasty rumors about him, anything. I settled for giving him a hard time with the kids. I turned them against him by presenting an image of him as a bum; I made it hard for him to see them; I tortured him through them.

"For the first year or two, my focus had been on self-pity and hate rather than on working to reorder my life. Gradually I calmed down and started to take care of myself. There were still hassles between Jon and me, twinges of jealousy still passed through me regarding his new family, but things were becoming reasonably civilized. I began to take care of my appearance; I went back to school and started to dance again. That's something I should have returned to years before—dancing; it had a marvelous effect on my well-being. I became increasingly determined to face the world not as the other half of Jon Richards or the parasitic other half of anyone, but as an independent, fully functioning human being. After two years or so, I had run out of my 'garbage' emotions and emerged from a difficult period. I discovered something very important: I can stand on my own two feet and make it!

"One of the nicest benefits of my journey was when I began to feel differently toward men, to see them as equals. Not better, not evil. This made dating and my relationship with my former husband and his family much less tense and complicated. For the first time the possibility of remarriage didn't seem to be a neurotic cop-out for me. Seeing that I could be all right without a man assured me that I could be successful with one."

Divorce need not be the signal that life has come to a halt and is never to be resumed. Janet Richards survived and eventually prospered. Many others—men, women, and children—have likewise succeeded in the face of broken marriages, despite the almost universal feeling among the divorced that rebuilding one's life is a hopeless task. Gradually, out of necessity, most lives will move toward coherence and order. With most people, though, the process of recovery is not likely to proceed without setbacks. Some days will pass easily and it will feel good to be alive; these may be followed by days filled with monumental distress where thoughts of suicide are not unusual. Some problems, the pragmatics of a new living arrangement, for example, may be resolved smoothly; others, such as developing a new social network, may not be solved for months. Some emotional issues may take much longer: Strong feelings toward the former mate, feelings of injustice, fear of making it alone and of new emotional involvements stubbornly refuse to vanish.

Dr. Robert S. Weiss, chairman of the Department of Sociology at the University of Massachusetts, in his book *Marital Separation* offers this view of the recovery process:

There appear to be two fairly distinct phases in movement toward recovery. One is a period of *transition* in which the pre-existent pattern of life has been disrupted and a new pattern not yet integrated. The first few months of this period of transition are for many a time of disorganization, depression, unmanageable restlessness, and chaotic searching for escape from distress. In later months individuals are more likely to display a determined attempt to regain their footing, to begin functioning again, and to return order to their lives.

Dr. Weiss goes on to describe a second phase, *recovery,* which, he suggests, evolves after eight or ten months of transition. During this second phase, the individual has established an equilibrium and may appear to function as well or better than before. However, he or she is still somewhat fragile and can expect to be rocked if a serious reversal occurs. This underlying frailty ordinarily diminishes as a stable and resilient new identity and pattern of life become increasingly established. The total process, Weiss reports, may take from two to four years.

Because of individual differences, Weiss's findings concerning the recovery period are likely to vary widely. Yet, whether the marriage dissolves through divorce or death, one lesson of the formerly married stands out clearly: Moving into a new marriage immediately is frequently a mistake. For most people, a difficult emotional struggle and a healing period are required, during which they may expect neither to love judiciously nor fully. Time is important, too—wounds close slowly. Support and sustained help from friends who not only offer a shoulder to cry on but also the reassurance that they wholly accept and value the aggrieved can help with the reconstruction process. Meaningful activities—social service, politics, college classes, and various self-improvement regimens—also prove beneficial for many people.

## Dating and Related Matters

Dating, for all the fears of rejection and questions of intimacy the term provokes in the formerly married, is a necessary element in the healing process. When emotions are wounded, there is, as with a broken limb, a period of knitting during which isolation is required; but if the limb is to grow strong again, it must be tested. Our feelings operate in similar fashion: We need to try them out, exercise them, even if cautiously at first, in order that they may return, in time, to full functioning.

Just as the first steps a patient may take after a long illness and confinement to bed may be shaky, the initial dating experience for most of the uncoupled is unsettling. Even the word "dating" is awkward, it sounds unnatural; the term seems more fitting to adolescents. When applied to the behavior of mature individuals who were married and who have children and responsibilities it is often felt to be offensive. "Dating," as one man expressed it, "conjures up an image of dancing at a disco, necking in a parked car, and grappling for romance on a couch. That was me at nineteen; at thirty-nine it feels pretty silly."

Despite the initial uneasiness with both term and practice, dating remains the most popular method of developing new romantic associations and evaluating the desirability of a continuing relationship. For these reasons, the great majority of people begin going out within the first year after the termination of their marriage. For some, the experience is, at best, mildly pleasant; for others, it is distressing—evenings of straining to make conversation, of trying to conceal boredom, grief, or anxiety, of plotting how to steal away without offending. But for most of the formerly married, after several dates—trial runs, of a sort—the experience is quite positive. One man's reaction:

"Meeting new people was a very potent antidote to the indoctrination imposed on me by my wife—'You are a cold, aloof, unlikable person.' I didn't really feel that way about myself, but I wondered at times, 'Could she be right?' If she was, I have changed dramatically or my coldness was in reaction to her because this has not been my experience with other women. I feel comfortable and natural offering myself without guile to many of my dates. I am pleased to find how communicative and outgoing I can be. Many of the women I have seen are easy to talk to, we discuss each other's feelings, neutral topics now and again, common interests, and the like. There is an easy flow that has developed after a few dating experiences. I have discovered latent social skills and personal charm I didn't even realize I possessed. Rather than a reminder of a tragedy—my torn marriage—dating has been educational, an important experience for me."

And this from a woman describing her dating experiences:

"I was very nervous when I first started dating. I got dressed so early for my first few dates that each time I had to change my blouse from perspiring too much. After so many years of being housewife and mother, I found it alarming that now I had to become mysterious and alluring, playgirl to some stranger. I didn't feel like a tantalizing, desirable female. I felt more like a used car! I worried about how to introduce my two boys, what to tell them, how they would react, what I would talk about, what to do about sex—I worried about everything.

"After five or six dates there was a gradual settling down. Meeting a new person became less frightening when it occurred to me that people are fundamentally the same. While I was worried about being judged, I hadn't considered that the other person was probably worrying that I was judging him. When I stopped preoccupying myself with my own uneasiness and instead put my date at ease, my discomfort disappeared. From there on, it became much more fun. I was no longer tongue-tied. I am amazed at how personal and intimate conversation can get in almost no time at all.

"On one date it started when I asked how old his kids were and he asked about mine and then asked how they were taking the loss of their father. I didn't mind him asking, and before I knew it, we were talking very personally about our marriages and our lives—things that I had expected to discuss only with close friends. Best of all, I didn't regret my experiences the next day. You know, the 'Why did you say that?' kind of thing. To the contrary, I felt a wave of warmth all through me."

One problem plaguing both men and women when they first begin dating is sex. Although some of the formerly married report sex to be a primary motivation for dating, lust is usually only one factor. Sex promises emotional fulfillment, security, reassurance, and intimacy—even if it doesn't always deliver. Unaccustomed to the practice of dating and often uncertain about others' intentions and their own wishes, the formerly married usually feel at a loss for guidelines to "appropriate" behavior. Before a date, both men and women are likely to speculate about the desirability of the relationship becoming sexual. Frequently they experience a tension that is specifically sexual: "Should it or will it become sexual? How is the decision to be made?"

Some men and women resolve the dilemma neatly by becoming indiscriminately sexual. They initiate a nearly ceaseless sexual hunt and a series of brief sexual affairs that reflect complex feelings: lust, a hope of gaining (or avoiding) a new love, reassurance of worth and attractiveness. The double standard, diluted but still operative, is a factor here. Not only are men more prone to this behavior but they react to it differently. Reflecting on these experiences, they are likely to boast about the time they "fucked everything in sight." Women, on the other hand, often refer to this aspect of their lives as confused and unhappy. Both men and women, when they eventually establish a firmer sense of themselves, find that the predicament of when and with whom to have sex returns in full force.

Among the guidelines that are established by some men and women is a premeditated ration of intimacies: The first date may include a kiss, the second sexual foreplay, the third date, if there is one, may include full sexuality. Others will permit a relationship to become sexual only if it is clear that love feelings are mutual or if it promises to become loving. Still others accept a sexual relationship with someone they find attractive regardless of the timing or the promise of a future. If societal mores are consulted for sexual policy, little help is found. In sexual matters, our culture remains divided and confused. In truth, most of us are ambivalent about our sexuality and do not know how to resolve the dilemma comfortably. Such ambiguity is perplexing for the person seeking certainty. Yet, for all the discomfort this may invoke, it points to the best source of direction—internal. Each individual ought to consult, not a timetable or a societal standard, but his or her feelings, and behave in whatever way is compatible with them. This, ultimately, proves to be the most reliable guide.

Along with confused feelings about sex and the initial strains of dating is an ambivalence as to its purpose. Although the ultimate goal for most is to find a potential replacement for the absent spouse, few are so one-sided in their intentions. Many, realizing that a new commitment would be premature, begin dating a variety of people in order to prevent one relationship from becoming all-important or exclusive. Under these circumstances, dating provides a diversion, a device for staving off loneliness, a sexual outlet, and most important, a way to gradually become acclimated to romantic relationships without the heavy burden and responsibility of loving. A young architect's attitude after eight months of postmarital dating:

"I hope someday to marry again, but right now I find seeing lots of different women to be stimulating, intellectually and sexually. It gives me the freedom not to have to go along with the personal predilections of someone else; the minute a woman starts to corner me and demands that I be this way or that, I back off. Seeing many women is, at present, protection for me. It's much easier to keep things noncommitted that way. Besides, I'm not ready to give up all the women who find me attractive and who drift in and out of my life. Loving is a luxury I am not quite ready for yet."

The use of dating to avoid involvement can take many forms. Often, as was the case above, variety is introduced as the safeguard. Some men and women choose married people as their dates to assure themselves of limited involvement. Others warn each of their dates not to expect commitment. Some men accomplish this by telling their dates that they consider themselves "free spirits"; some women in an equivalent maneuver discourage continuity by being "busy" on numerous occasions if too much interest is shown. For many, limiting the amount of time they spend with any one date is the strategy of choice. Even if they reveal their innermost feelings and are warm, they do so in a controlled manner, arranging not to see the person again for several weeks after each disclosure.

Behaving in this fashion—avoiding emotional intimacy or seeking it in limited doses—is not symptomatic of poor functioning. For most people, it is an integral part of the natural healing process. If dating never proceeds beyond the beginning stages of wariness and limited involvement, more often than not the obstacles take the form of contrivances that conceal a feeling of low self-regard.

## Contrivances to Avoid

While most of us want love in the form of a special person to enter our life, we also fear—particularly after a failed marriage—that we may be found undesirable. For some people, this fear of rejection results in the formation of a false front, a mask to avoid being known. Hidden behind this mask is usually the belief, conscious or implicit, that to be one's real self is dangerous, that exposure of real feelings will lead to being unwanted: "If people found out what I was really like, they wouldn't want any part of me." One woman who felt this way described in a therapy session one of the masks she had been using, and how confused and empty she had become regarding her own convictions:

"I was thinking about the tension I experience on dates. It occurred to me that I have developed a knack for determining what kind of person a man likes and then pretending to be that person. This seems to put my companions at ease, but since they have an inaccurate concept of me, I am left with the burden of maintaining the phoniness. At parties I could be lively and appear to be having a good time but all the while I'd be putting on a little drama, creating the illusion that I am bright and interesting so that men will be attracted. Sometimes I'd even surprise myself by arguing against what I really thought when I saw that somebody I wanted to impress would be quite unhappy about it if I didn't. It's been so long since I stood up for my convictions that I don't know whether I still have convictions to stand up for. I haven't been honestly myself. I don't actually know what my real self is; I've been just playing a lot of false roles.

". . . I even went so far as to break off an engagement with a very special man because I was sure that someone that fantastic could not possibly love me once we started to live together and he really got to know me. Instead, I sought out somebody I felt to be inferior because I was more comfortable with him. He was safer. Yet, I was dissatisfied with that relationship because I didn't really care for the guy. It seems if I'm attracted to somebody, I louse it up by caring too much about pleasing them. Or I become involved with men who don't please me. In the two years since my divorce, I have continued in the same pattern: I get into relationships that I end if I feel myself getting too close to someone who really appeals to me, or I spend more time than I want with men who say they are turned on to me but toward whom I feel nothing."

This woman is beginning to discover that her behavior and even the feelings she experiences do not flow naturally from her genuine reactions, but are a façade behind which she has been hiding. She is discovering how much of her life is guided by what she thinks she *should* be rather than by what she is. Still more disturbing, she recognizes that she exists in response to the demands of others, that she seems to have no direction of her own. Below are some other façades constructed to attract affection or, failing that, to avoid rejection. All have in common the element of inauthenticity.

## The Judges

The individual who feels "I am no good" but protectively transforms this into *"They* are no good" provides negative insurance in the event of a rejection: "Well, he (she) was offensive anyway!" The Judges and their correlates, the Comparers, Convictors, Blamers, and Resentment Collectors do not feel comfortable with a new person until they have found a blemish. While carefully scanning the new person for a defect, these people are careful to avoid any intimacy that might expose one of their own faults. Their relationships with others are not tolerant and accepting but are characterized by a zealous concern with what sort of behavior is "appropriate," "indecent," and "offensive."

## The Nice Guys

These people exaggerate their caring and love; they kill with kindness. They are chameleons who hardly ever disagree, who convince themselves to be whatever the other person in the relationship wants, even though that may violate their own integrity. For the illusion that they are loved, they give up their self-respect. After all, they silently hope, who can reject a Nice Guy!

## The Conquerors

Using charm, wit, and flirtation, Conquerors signal their availability and derive great pleasure and excitement from rigorous social/sexual pursuit. Since they feel hostile toward and damaged by members of the opposite sex, as soon as the "pursued" is committed, the Conquerors' interest drops. The primary gratification comes from having acquired another "conquest trophy" and, to some degree, through revenge for past hurts by being the "rejector."

## The Feelers

Just as some people are closed and nonexpressive, others go to the opposite extreme and use indiscriminate openness and the expression of what they call "genuine feelings" to gain affection and love. In its more comical form, the expression of such a "genuine feeling" may be preceded by an announcement that it is on its way. After the announcement, the feeling is described, or rather presented, as though it were a rare and profound offering that should be exhibited in the National Feeling Show. Often Feelers tell their entire life story, all problems included, on the first date.

## Male/Female Chauvinist

*All* interpersonal difficulties are part of a plot by the opposite sex to oppress, control, or psychologically destroy their counterparts: "My wife's (husband's) problem was that she (he) basically hated men (women) and was out to prove their inferiority." Rather than approaching people with an open, unbiased view, the Chauvinists take a stereotyped, politicized stance. Having found a simplistic answer that absolves them of any psychological failure, they interpret and explain everything in this manner. A typical comment: "The reason my sexual advances are rejected is that women are too busy competing with men these days." Men who take a Chauvinist position are likely to whistle at, talk down to, and attempt to dominate women. Women are likely to feel *consistently* sexualized, to be humorless, and constantly to challenge even the slightest hint of unfairness in their dating relations. Both men and women who hold to this rigid posture are, at base, afraid of each other.

## The Swingers

Sex is the answer—regardless of the question. Sex is the cure for everything, particularly loneliness: "It is impossible for two people to know each other intimately if they haven't been sexual," Swingers insist. Reject a Swinger and you'll be told you have a hang-up. Accept the Swinger's terms for getting to know one another more "intimately," and it is likely you will soon find him or her off "swinging" with someone else in an attempt to "get to know *them* better." The Swinger, in a misguided effort to develop a loving relationship with someone, puts sexual priorities before emotional ones and consequently finds something missing; feeling a vague dissatisfaction, he or she dismisses it as "bad vibes" and goes off to another bed. And another and another and another.

Whether an individual masquerades in one of the false faces described or chooses another—that of the Suffering Stoic, the Wounded Idealist, the Witty Comic, the Innocent Victim, or the

Rueful Sinner—doesn't matter. Whether people conceal themselves in this manner or behind banter, name dropping, or business talk, the result is the same. All facades—cover-ups for the fear that we are unworthy as we are—defeat the possibility of a new, lasting love relationship. It is only natural to want to be liked and appreciated by other people; "wearing a disguise" in order to accomplish this, however, ultimately inhibits intimacy and results in self-alienation. Those who are stuck in this behavior, not as an occasional role, but as a continuing, repetitive pattern, may go to parties, date a great deal, and even have numerous affairs, but essentially they remain unrevealed, and hence unconnected.

Frequently, when people relate in a contrived manner there are signals to this effect. An atmosphere of strain, artificiality, anxiety, and tension prevails. The contact leaves one feeling empty, it is not nourishing. In contrast, authentic interpersonal behavior is not effortful, planned, or deliberately assumed. Rather, it is spontaneous and unpremeditated. Such behavior, in the long run, turns out to be flexible and versatile; the contact feels good, it is fulfilling.

## Readiness for New Relationships

In postmarital life, as in everything else, those who are better prepared have an advantage. Individuals in this circumstance may need to call on resources of many kinds, social, personal and financial. The more such resources exist, or the sooner they can be established, the better off the individual is likely to be.

Those who have a strong sense of inner security, competence in a marketable skill, who have a cadre of loyal and supportive people in their lives, in addition to adequate financial resources, are best off. They are likely to be ready to pursue new relationships soon—perhaps only days or weeks after the marriage is broken. In contrast, the man or woman whose personality integration is fragile, who has a tendency to panic in response to frustration, will, irrespective of other circumstances, find postmarital distress much more difficult to manage and consequently be less ready—although more needy—regarding new relationships.

For those less advantaged—individuals prone to the interpersonal contrivances discussed earlier, for instance—psychotherapy might be considered to help remove impediments to full recovery. One indication that psychotherapy is warranted, aside from pretense in cross-sex relationships, is frequent and intense upset beyond the first few months of separation. In these instances, the goals of the therapy or self-help process should include not only the critical factor—modification of attitudes that stand as obstacles to healthier functioning—but specific guidelines with regard to the recovery process. There are several factors discussed by Dr. Robert Weiss in his book *Marital Separation* that might be considered:

### Living Arrangements

Both men and women who have recently separated may sometimes find that temporarily returning to their parents' home eases the strain. There they need not be completely self-reliant and can gradually regain their bearings. In a more secure environment, panic may subside and allow an opportunity for growth toward increased independence. For the husband or wife with child custody, grandparents can provide needed help and support for the children. The risk here is that a serious conflict of authority with regard to the children may develop or inappropriate constraints may be imposed on the uncoupled by their parents. As a compromise, it may be better not to establish coresidence but to move nearby, thus gaining the advantages of accessibility while avoiding the constraint of too much closeness. Such arrangements can also be made with other relatives or close friends.

### Reestablishing Community

For the most part ours is a coupled society. Being unmarried, sadly, often results in feeling like an outsider, a marginal individual. Married friends no longer seem to have the same interests and concerns and there is a feeling of being a social misfit. One's sense of belonging, an important factor for a satisfactory life, is damaged; membership in a valued network helps fend off social isolation.

Although some people find postmarital groups—Parents Without Partners and other singles groups of various kinds—unsatisfying and feel further alienated by them, these groups offer valuable advantages that should not be dismissed without consideration. They are easily entered and usually provide an atmosphere of compassion and friendliness to newcomers; they provide members with social linkages that are less available elsewhere. Because the people drawn to these organizations have shared a similar life experience, fellow members are able to provide each other with support and understanding.

Some organizations also offer services of a practical nature. Many chapters of Parents Without Partners, for example, have developed children's programs on weekends and holidays so that men and women who have their children at that time have a place to take them. Even for those who are reluctant to join an organization for the formerly married, there are advantages: It is a useful stopover while gradually exploring other areas of involvement—sporting clubs, avocational pursuits, and the like.

## Employment

Among the benefits of employment, aside from money, is access to a community of fellow employees. This not only increases a person's social network, but provides a very useful sense of belonging and productivity. For women who were not employed at the termination of their marriage, it is an option worth considering.

Employment can be especially valuable to women who have previously defined themselves as "housewife." For them, the end of the marriage is equivalent to having been fired, though some, of course, have quit! In any case, going to work can expand one's self-definition and put one in contact with a community where new friendships can be made that extend into nonwork life. Having a job offers other advantages. It can counteract a tendency toward withdrawal into household chores; it provides a meaningful place to go. Employment can be so therapeutic and growth-enhancing that even mothers of small children would be wise to explore the possibilities. Part-time employment with adequate provision made for children is unlikely to harm the children and quite likely to result in a valuable asset for their mother.

While some people suffer deeply during the postmarital period, requiring substantial time and aid to recover, and others sprint forward almost immediately, most individuals fall between these two extremes. Sooner or later, though, a desire begins to grow for new relationships. This desire is bound to be frustrated if the rehabilitation process has been seriously impeded, but assuming psychological readiness, the following guidelines can smooth the way for new relationships:

1. *Do not assume you know a person after a first meeting.* It takes time to expose the wide range of feelings and behavior available to us; since most people are wary initially, first impressions are often misleading—or, at the least, quite incomplete. Although relationships require time to blossom, some people—to their disadvantage—insist that they can assess what another person is like on the basis of a brief party acquaintanceship or dinner date. Diane, for example, will not go out with the same man twice if he doesn't "prove" that he is an interesting person on the first date. Steven cuts women out of his life if they do not immediately respond to his sexual advances. There are many men and women who see in a new acquaintance a slight resemblance to their ex-spouse, and instantly dislike this person because of it. All these people are missing out on "could-have-been" relationships because of silly prejudice.

2. *Just as a snap judgment is often self-defeating, it is also foolish to pursue persistently someone who isn't interested in you.* Relationships involve a complex interplay of values, in-

terests, and physical attraction; many people simply do not match and never will. Aside from incompatibility, some people either have other demands on their time and, literally, don't have time for you, or they are defensive, overly shy, and generally unavailable. In these instances, it is wise to accept these others as the strangers they wish to be so that you have the time and energy to develop relationships with people who desire you.

3. *Discard any preconceived timetable for meeting a compatible person or for developing a close relationship with that person.* This point is particularly critical: The surest guarantee that a relationship will collapse is to impose, in advance, a prescribed period of time for it to flourish.

4. *Learning to relate closely again is bound to be unsettling.* Anxiety is likely to be a part of this experience. Rather than automatically regarding this emotion as a signal to back away, reconsider: Do you want to go on protecting yourself or do you want to develop a new relationship? If you want the latter, it is important to recognize that intimacy always involves some risk; consequently, anxiety is to be expected. Most rewarding relationships do not proceed smoothly.

5. *There is an oft-quoted but rarely appreciated biblical phrase: "Do unto others as you would have others do unto you."* People who abide by this code are more likely to develop satisfying relationships. Indeed, those who are chronically unhappy with other people probably are so because of a failure to see others as similar, in many respects, to themselves. Most of us want the same things in our relationships: honesty, a sharing of feelings and thoughts, empathy, support, fun. Those of us who are not getting these qualities from others might ask: "Do I myself offer these same things to others?" There is no guarantee that being a model of what you want will produce positive results, but the probabilities increase very dramatically. How, then, do you improve your chances of attaining a close relationship? The answer is simple. *You* attempt to move closer to the person, you take him or her into *your* confidence and share *your* thoughts and feelings.

# 3 Previous Attachments: Terminable and Interminable

## The Persistence of Former Love

While new love is especially joyous, former love is resilient. Even though severed through decree or mortal destiny, it lingers on and endures in one form or another. For the widowed, loyalty to the dead spouse may present an almost intangible barrier to love feelings, at least for a time. In many instances—particularly when the remaining partner is young—a period of convalescence brings perspective and the former partnership is, in effect, canceled. In contrast with the finality of death, divorce, though it nullifies the partnership between man and woman, does not entirely erase the bond. As long as practical matters exist between ex-spouses—alimony, which signifies the penalty of failure; and children, flesh-and-blood reminders of the former attachment—they continue to be indissolubly linked.

Childless persons, of course, have less holding them together. Yet even here emotional sparks linger and are apt to ignite upon the news that a former spouse is deeply involved with someone or is remarrying. Arthur Mead, twenty-eight and divorced two years, found this to be true.

## Previous Attachments

"I ran into her in an expensive restaurant. I was alone, treating myself to a good meal after a particularly trying day. She was waiting for a table, hanging on this guy's arm, looking her very best; her hair was soft, shiny; she was dressed carefully and looking quite elegant. When she spotted me, we both turned away, trying to deny each other's presence. Finally, as she was being shown to her table, she stopped and introduced him. She looked at him in a very sweet, tender way. I knew it was serious.

"Funny—after the introduction I changed my order and ordered something more expensive. I guess I sort of needed an extra boost. A few weeks later I heard they were married. It was really strange. When we were married, we were miserable; I didn't want her back, but inside I felt jolted. I was really taken aback by the wave of emotion that swept over me."

Reactions such as Arthur Mead's—emptiness infused with surprise—can be transitory; they are the last steps in a nearly completed inner rehabilitation process. For some people, though—those who married in order to avoid becoming autonomous individuals, the insecure, and those who are afraid to try to meet others—reactions to a former mate's serious involvement or remarriage signals a more ominous message: enslavement by the past, hidden feelings of proprietorship, and continuing emotional dependency. To become an individual, to loosen the habit of seeing oneself as part of a couple, requires learning to live without somebody to lean on. Some people have forgotten how to do it; others have never learned. For these people, months or even years after the separation, the former spouse is apt to remain the most important figure in their world. The lost lover remains vivid in the individual's focus, there to be pestered, threatened, and called on to witness the devastation produced by the divorce.

The presence of children provides the man or woman who is still emotionally bound to a former mate a ready excuse for continuance. Some individuals telephone the former spouse endlessly under the pretense of discussing their offspring: "Mark had such a marvelous day; Alice is joining gymnastics."

Sometimes, the calls, announcing a minor episode, come quite late at night; these are the transparently veiled attempts to interrupt any intimacy that may be taking place: "I hope I'm not disturbing you, but I wanted you to know that Anne got her cooking badge in Brownies today." In other instances, the pretense is a pseudoproblem: "I don't know what we are going to do about Mark's table manners; just the other day . . ." On still other occasions, a former partner may summon the child's parent to frequent meetings for the manifest purpose of discussing urgent parenting matters—and use the opportunity to flirt with a hidden agenda: reuniting.

"Brenda had been calling about the children constantly. Although it seemed as if things were going as well as could be expected with them—and she was overreacting, as usual—I reluctantly agreed to meet with her. She insisted we meet on 'neutral' ground. 'Neutral' turned out to be a quiet, dimly-lit French restaurant with an unmistakable romantic ambiance. Brenda was wearing the perfume she knows I like, her hair was pushed back carefully; she looked her very best. After a rather alcoholic lunch made tolerable by small talk—without mention of the children—she blurted out, 'Do you want to talk about what went wrong?' She knew I was about to be married, I couldn't believe she'd be so bold—and told her so.

"Brenda just sat there in stony silence, her eyes welled up with tears. Then she said, 'Well, I just thought that we ought to discuss it and decide if we did the right thing.' She began sobbing and dabbing at her eyes with a handkerchief; 'I'm really lonely,' she wept, 'I have nobody.' With that, as if she had just been confronted with her unspoken misery—hearing it out loud like that—she grew angry, her outpouring of sorrow turned to a seething rage, and she stormed out of the restaurant. I just sat there in shock. I was assailed by guilt. I knew she was saying, 'I need you.' It was a desperate attempt to reconciliate. Maybe all I had to do was be nice to her; I could've avoided the question and maybe she wouldn't have become so upset. I felt incredibly guilty. That night I had an enormous fight with Nora, my wife-to-be. I know it was my anguish; I couldn't stand myself."

Sometimes it is the woman who is bound by guilt and pity to her ex-mate, but more often, as in the case above, it is the man. Unfair though it is, the ex-wife is commonly more obligated by her role as custodial parent; consequently, she has less opportunity for new relationships and is generally more fearful that the passage of time will dim her attractiveness and result in enduring isolation. Whoever strains at the thought of a former spouse remarrying creates new issues that demand resolution.

## Remarriage: Adverse Reactions

That ex-spouses *must* adversely affect a remarriage is a myth. Yet it is indisputable that when one partner of a broken marriage remarries and one does not, there is a swelling of disruptive emotions. This surge of emotion may be based largely on pragmatics: Women are more often financially dependent on their husbands than self-supporting. On hearing of her husband's plans, a woman is apt to fear a loss of economic assistance; she may worry that the financial drain of a new family is going to produce a money squeeze that will make the payment of alimony and child support increasingly distasteful to him. Frequently her worst fears are realized. The resentment over these payments does indeed influence a husband's continuing support. The ex-wife's reaction may be to involve him in legal proceedings that will be disruptive to his new life. Thus alimony may be seen by the remarried husband as destructive to his remarriage in two ways: If he delays or stops payment, he may have legal problems with his former wife; but if he continues payment, it will be financial hardship that the present wife may grow to resent. One husband put it this way:

"It seems as though I've been bled dry by financial obligations all my life. Jane married me, but I know she sometimes gets very disheartened by all my encumbrances. She sees money go out to my former wife that we need for our own very trimmed budget, and she resents it. One time she just blurted it out: 'I wish your other family would just go away and leave us alone!' I can't say I blame her. But when I don't send the agreed upon sum of money, my ex-wife calls me and we fight. This arouses all the old feelings of hurt and anger in both of us and I feel terrible for days."

His present wife offers her view:

"I think I resent his ex-wife mostly because of my inability to have children with him. We would both like another child, but because of the financial obligations, it is utterly impossible. This is a very tough issue for me to accept. Rationally or not, I blame her for my deprivation. She is working now and I feel she does not need the same amount of alimony. I am not questioning the child support—that's legitimate; but dammit, the alimony should be reduced. To top it off, I feel that my husband is still feeling guilty and that is why he isn't putting up more of a fight. If that's true, it's not very reassuring to me."

On another level, remarriage may provoke in a woman—or a man, for that matter—a piercing feeling of rejection. The former spouse's remaining emotional loyalty has been removed; now he or she belongs completely to someone else. The former wife may appear to be indifferent or jokingly hostile upon her husband's remarriage ("Now someone else can experience the torture of living with Mrs. Roth's little boy!") when in fact she is jealous that someone else has won where she has lost. To compensate, the former husband may become too solicitous toward his ex-wife, whom he feels is now weak and alone, or, if he left her unwillingly, he may become very actively hostile in victory, expressing by his actions, "That'll show you what a mistake you made; I hope you rot in loneliness!"

Her jealousy, and the checking up on him through children and friends that often accompany it, is bound to fuel the fire: "How dare you spy on me; you are no longer a part of my life!" With this, a harsh and damaging attack, the former wife may feel everyone is ganging up on her—not only her ex-spouse, but the children who continue to visit their father and his new family. A strong need for revenge may develop; she may instigate vicious gossip, make outrageous financial demands, or, if nothing else works, prevent the children from seeing their remarried father. One woman who did all of these things, in the grip of anger, explained in retrospect her destructive course:

"I did not want a divorce; I was forced into it. There didn't seem to be any justice to compensate for being thrown aside. The negotiating process through the lawyers not only failed to abate my feelings, it perpetuated them. He and I despised each other so, we couldn't speak a sentence to each other on any subject. Each month when I received his check I felt insulted. I thought to myself, 'We worked together, dreamed together, now I get crumbs, while she, that bastard, reaps the rewards of his success.' I tried demeaning her to our friends, to his family ('This is what your precious son traded me in for'), and to the children. I wanted the children to give her a hard time. I threatened to take him into court to seek more money. It was a device to hurt him and them.

"I told the children that their father obviously doesn't love them because he deserted them and provides me with very little money. I succeeded in my efforts so well that his visits with them were sheer misery because they were so sullen and hostile. My oldest boy—he's fifteen—wouldn't talk to him at all. I convinced him that his father was a thoroughly bad and selfish man. He feels his father was rotten to leave me. When my husband yelled at him and told him he couldn't behave that way toward him, he just slammed the phone down and refused to answer any of his calls. This was my ultimate victory ... or so I thought.

"A year or so after his remarriage, two things happened that altered the course of things. A new man entered my life, which was timely—I was so lonely—and I began to notice the children were becoming self-doubting and insecure, entirely dependent on me. Difficulties were apparent in school. I took a long, hard look at my behavior, my wretched anger, and I saw something very ugly. I felt quite ashamed. The real losers in this masochistic war I was waging were the children. The truly punished was not my husband, but my children, particularly the fifteen-year-old, who I know has a well-hidden longing for his father."

Men, of course, are quite as capable of destructive behavior as women. Through seemingly casual questioning a father may recruit the children as spies: "Is your mother going out much? Is she treating you alright? Does anyone stay overnight?" After her remarriage, he may promote unfair comparisons between himself and his wife's new mate, hoping—though not admitting, even to himself—that this will create havoc. He asks his questions and drops his disparagements with a façade of innocence, but since he knows it will be reported, it is, in fact, a thinly disguised vehicle for transmitting to his former wife his continuing control over her. Again, the children suffer; as go-betweens, they are tugged by loyalty conflicts ("Should I tell him? Should I tell her?") and are more harmed than the one for whom the message is intended.

When his ex-wife remarries, a man who misses the day-to-day relationship with his children may find himself set back even further in regard to them. He cannot spend as much time with them in their new family, and his apartment is likely to be cramped, so his visits frequently have to take place on neutral ground. A museum, a movie, or a park are suitable for an occasional afternoon but both father and offspring are likely to rebel against this as a regular diet. If, as is often the case, he is tired, busy in his job, and has limited funds, he may be frustrated even further in his efforts to achieve a relationship with his children.

## The Noncustodial Connection

When the father does not see his children very much or sees them but relates to them stiffly—because of the unresolved tensions of the broken marriage, the offspring are likely to become resentful and exert their own pressures. To assuage his guilt feelings, a man may feel compelled to remarry and reorganize his life within the framework of a new family. His hope is that when his children visit him in his new home with his new wife, the artificial conditions under which they have been meeting will be reduced.

It is unwise (and uncommon) for a man to remarry for the sake of his children. The all too frequent alternative to remarriage chosen by the ex-husband embroiled in an emotional battle with his former wife is to stop caring, if possible, about his relationship with his children. He attempts, in effect, a partial emotional suicide to subdue the pain. Unable to surmount the antagonism being directed toward him, he gives up his relationship with the children. The same may be true, of course, for the divorced woman, and even more so, as more and more women lose or turn over custody to their husbands.

One woman's experience:

"I left my husband for another man. It was a very messy, even brutal situation for many months. Finally my husband agreed to a divorce only if he maintained custody of our two daughters. I had very mixed feelings about this but he claimed to have hard evidence of adultery that he would use in a long-drawn-out custody battle, so I eventually conceded. Now when I want to see the children, he makes it very difficult. It is my right to visit with them every weekend and he is not supposed to ask any questions, but as it is, I feel very intimidated by him. He probes endlessly: 'You getting married yet? Will the kids see you in bed with that guy? What kind of treatment do they get from him?' I suppose I feel guilty about what has happened. Somehow I feel obligated to keep quiet and play along. The end result is that I don't have (my) children anymore."

While some of the formerly married who do not have custody reluctantly give up their relationship with their children—because they find themselves powerless to reverse hostile or jealous interactions with their ex-mate—and others just vanish, seemingly without cause, or make contact only sporadically, the majority continue, as visiting parents, to have regular contact with their offspring. In most instances, the visiting parent experiences feelings of loss, powerlessness, frustration, and guilt. Thomas Robeson, age thirty-five, a man who two years ago chose to leave his wife of twelve years, explains:

"My children come to visit under considerable strain. My son Jason, aged seven, is very antagonistic, picking up the hostility from his mother. He acts bitter and obnoxious. My two girls are a little older and are less of a problem. In my opinion, Jason's hostility is a direct reflection of his mother's feelings and it is tied in with her emotional insecurity and her expression of her fears to the children. Jason seems to take it the hardest and there doesn't seem to be anything I can do about it. He has become so disturbed about his mother's problem that he has, on several occasions, accused my present wife, Doris, of stealing me. He is particularly cruel to her. It is a very disturbing situation. I don't know how it will be resolved. Each weekend Jason comes over—it's surprising that he would want to be with us—and despite the anticipatory tension in Doris and me, things begin all right. Then, bang, there's an explosion of rage. I know Jason is hurting; maybe I'm at fault; I'm not sure anymore. But one thing I know is that Vivian has made no attempt to protect the children from her venom and that's damn destructive. She claims they have to learn about life, but I see that as a lame excuse for vindictiveness. Meanwhile the kids are being damaged...."

Another dilemma for the noncustodial parent occurs when

the former mate remarries. The stepparent is the day-to-day caretaker in the home with the children. The noncustodial parent has, of course, no say as to who this person will be. A father may hear another man being referred to as Daddy; it may be made difficult for him to see the children; a loss of control is likely to be intensely felt. It hurts. One man, Ronald Mayer, reacted to his pain by denouncing his wife as irresponsible:

"'Look,' I told her, 'as long as I'm providing child support, Roger is going to be dressed and groomed in a style I deem proper. I don't know what kind of a joker you married, what kind of example he sets, but Roger is not to be walking around needing a haircut, with holes in his pants and torn sneakers. He looks like a bum. Every time I pick him up, you're off somewhere, and he is dirty—dirty clothes and dirty face. What kind of home are you and this guy providing for him? It's just like you to become so romantically engrossed that Roger falls by the wayside.... And another thing, I absolutely will not stand for Roger calling him Daddy. I know this is happening because Roger admitted it. Goddamnit, Grace, I am his father. He may be your husband, but Roger is my kid!'"

In a calmer moment, Mr. Mayer speaks of his despair:

"Actually, it was good that Grace remarried. I don't feel all that horrible about it but I am very attached to my son and I don't know where or how to get myself over the loss. Complaining about his grooming was bullshit. I think Grace realized that. It's just that I ache over that kid. Sometimes I just dial their number automatically to hear his voice. On some of these calls, Roger is bubbling over and eager to talk. Other times, he's busy with a friend, or eating dinner, or watching television, and doesn't want to stay on the phone. I try to understand and not feel slighted but it's difficult; I miss him so much."

Obviously, a weekly or biweekly visit of several hours does not provide the same continuity of awareness as living within the same household. By the time the noncustodial parent meets with his children, the events and crises that occurred in the interval since the last meeting will have been nearly forgotten. And even if the children do remember to say that they were kept after school one day, or received an award of merit, being reported to is not the same as being present when an event was first emotionally experienced. Beyond the lack of continuity, however, as Ronald Mayer makes clear, is the fact that the noncustodial parent is no longer counted on as a source of support. The remaining parent and his or her spouse become the guiding, nurturing, protecting adults to the children. It is to them that they turn for daily assistance.

## Entanglements to Avoid

One would think that uncoupled parents have an imperative to work out the details of their postmarital relationship—if only for the children's sake. This is so, yet unlike the childless couple who engage an attorney to work out the arrangements and so bypass a personal confrontation, parents are offered a destructive but nonetheless richly tempting opportunity to continue the emotional war that began when the marriage was intact. If the marital and divorce experiences were major battles, in the postmarital relationship, the children can become hosts to border skirmishes. Often, the attacks are waged under the protective, unassailable guise of selfless parental concern.

The following telephone conversation in which the issue slides from the children to "Don't you feel guilty" illustrates one technique.

SHE: Well, I'd think you'd want your children to take music lessons since they seem to have some talent in this area. After all, you promised to pay for all educational expenses.

HE: I can't afford any extra expenses right now. Music lessons will have to wait. I'm supporting all of you, I have a new family to provide for, another house to pay for; I'm strapped.

SHE: And whose fault is that?

HE: Look, Gloria, let's not get into it.

SHE: *(provocatively)* What do you mean, "Let's not get into it!" You leave your family, pick up with another family, and then tell me you want to penalize your children—and I'm supposed to be merry!

HE: *(angered, feeling guilty)* I'm not penalizing them, I just can't afford it right now

SHE: If you shout, I'm afraid I'll have to hang up. Let's just talk calmly about this. Now, when are you going to stop fussing over somebody else's kids and reorder your allegiance?

HE: Oh, shit! *(click)*

Another common entanglement, more an indication of underlying hostility than parental concern, occurs when one or both partners strike at each other with complaints about parenting performance:

HE: Ginger looks terrible. She's pale, anemic looking. Are you too busy running around to feed her properly? You always were lax about bedtime rules. She looks as if she's not getting enough sleep. What the hell is going on? Can't you do anything right?

SHE: She told me she saw you and what's-her-name in bed together. I will not permit her to visit you if you do not use more discretion. I don't care how you explain it away. If Ginger is unprotected from your perversity, I will contact my lawyer and haul you into court.

HE: Listen, you must really be crazy! That woman is my wife. What the hell is wrong with Ginger knowing that I am happily in love. Christ, you would think we were screwing in front of her or something. But what does

that have to do with her looking so washed out?
SHE: It's you she's disturbed about, not me. You're the one who's draining her.

Some combative parents intervene directly, setting the child against their ex-mate by contradicting their child-rearing procedures: "I don't care what your mother says about eating candy. I'm the one who pays the dental bills and I'm telling you that candy is out! You stop chewing on that gum, and that's all there is to it. And you can tell your mother that's the new rule!" Others play the game differently. Without acknowledging hostility, a wife may present any impenetrable excuse for not having the children available on a day their father had hoped to see them: "They insisted on visiting my mother for a few days so I sent them off this morning." When the husband does arrange to see the children, the wife may insist that he tell her his plans for the day in detail, thus communicating her exclusive proprietorship of the children. The wife may further reinforce the notion of her husband's loss by insisting that he see the children in *her* home in *her* presence, saying, in effect, "You are no longer in control."

Husbands, too, have their arsenal of weapons. A man may do his utmost to indulge his children's whims for toys and the like so that they realize the poverty of their lives with their mother, or treat them as especially responsible and mature so they will be stung by the contrast with their mother's more protective handling. He may not show up when his wife—and children—expect him, or be consistently inflexible on those occasions he does appear, timing his visits so that they disrupt plans for the children made by their stepparent or returning the children at grossly inconvenient hours.

One man, for example, told his wife each week at what hour he would be returning the children, but sometimes arrived punctually, other times quite early, leaving the youngsters home alone, and still other times several hours late. This not only worried the children's mother, but effectively spoiled her and her present husband's plans for the day. No amount of pleading by his ex-wife or gentle intervention by her present husband convinced this man—torn by the indignity of losing his children to another man—to modify his behavior. He buttressed himself against all accusation: "But this is my time with the children—wouldn't you agree that it is important for them to have a good relationship with their *real* father? You know, I can't be blamed if things don't always go as planned for you and your husband. Why don't you both try therapy . . . ?"

In addition to the relationship between the formerly coupled, remarriage enlarges the cast of characters. There may be new front-line combatants, since new and former spouses can grate on each other in subtle ways. There is the tendency to make comparisons: "Am I a better lover than my predecessor? Am I brighter? Do I live up to expectations?" Both husbands and wives are tempted to influence their present spouses to become support troops. A present wife thinks her predecessor is stupid, or greedy, or deceitful. She offers her assessment to her husband with hopes of reassuring confirmation. Not receiving it, she is disappointed: "Does he still have love feelings for her? Where is his loyalty? Is he unhappy with me?" A former wife reports her uncomplimentary opinion of her successor to mutual friends, knowing the word will get back and be disruptive. A new husband avoids certain routines because he knows they invite memories of his wife's former lover. The vibrations are ghosts that chill the warmest of moods.

As well as looking to their present partner as an ally in their war, the formerly married may worry about the influence of their ex's husband or wife on the children; they are often jealous and act to prevent a relationship. Husbands may intensify their sport or entertainment activities with their children and invite insidious comparison: "I'll bet your mother's husband [not stepfather!] doesn't play ball with you like that." They may encourage poking fun at the present husband in an effort to be divisive: "He certainly walks funny—What is he? Just too fat, or what?" The new wife may feel a natural inclination to befriend, advise, and nurture her husband's children who live with their mother but visit on weekends. Her demonstration of affection, if reported back to their mother, however, can antagonize and threaten her: "Don't you dare try to unsurp my role. You're not their mother, so just lay off!" Some take a similar position, but ambiguously. They allow the children plenty of exposure to their former mate's new family, particularly when they need a "baby sitter," but complain if the children are disciplined or treated in a parental manner by the stepparent. Others play out yet another of the endless "child-as-weapon" variations but keep solidly to the same destructive theme: "I will capture the final, bloody victory in this war."

## Reconciliation—of Sorts

"Can we be civilized about this?" a former couple ask each other. "Can we act sensibly?" they wonder silently. "Or are we to be enchained by entanglements that invariably perpetuate ill-will? How does one cope with a relationship as intense yet as ambivalent as the postmarital relationship of husbands and wives? Many former spouses prefer simply to drop the requirement; at one time or another, usually in a moment of desperation—when the guilt and anger press to unbearable limits—they may seek relief by fantasizing the demise of their antagonist. "I wish," one tormented woman sighed, "he would drop dead—painlessly, but instantly and thoroughly!"

Beyond wishful thinking, moving away is often considered as a solution. Relocating cannot erase past memories but it can halt the accumulation of new daily assaults. However, although it does produce a solution of sorts, reestablishing oneself elsewhere has serious drawbacks. For the noncustodial parent, contact with the children is, in effect, ended. Emotionally, this is often traumatic. For the custodial parent, it may be legally impossible to move a great distance away. Combine this with the loss of friends and family, starting over in a new job, and living in unfamiliar surroundings, and the psychological impact is almost intolerable. Because of the children, out of loneliness or a fear of rootlessness—for all the reasons already mentioned

—husbands and wives continue to exist in each other's lives and opportunities for harming each other are plentiful. Feelings are likely to be mixed and may alternate between friendship and animosity, or the two may be present simultaneously as in the man or woman who experiences both distress and relief upon the notice of a spouse's impending marriage.

An actively malevolent man or woman creates the most havoc—and there are limitations to defense. A court order can keep a man from physically harassing his wife's new husband, but what can keep him from subtly undermining this new man's authority in the house? What's to keep a woman from setting the children against their father? Fortunately, although there are no safeguards against these abuses, in most divorced persons, the feelings of anger, guilt, and yearning gradually shrivel. The average duration appears to be about two years—a difficult and seemingly endless period when what one desires is immediate surcease. Yet there are no shortcuts. It took time to weave so complicated a relationship and, despite impatience, the time requirement refuses to yield to emotional discomfort.

Along with time, disengagement from a former attachment depends to some extent on external circumstances. In this regard, some of the remarried, or those considering this path, are more fortunate than others. Young people who have former spouses, children from both marriages, and heavy support payments begin with more problems than older couples whose children are grown and living elsewhere. If a former partner is no longer alive, or lives a great distance away, relationships are simplified. Couples without children who both have careers can more easily disentangle their involvement, particularly if there is no demand for alimony, and can go their very separate ways. Community acceptance, including supportive rather than provocative intervention from friends, and neutrality on the part of former in-laws can also help to dissipate animosity.

Beyond circumstantial factors—often lying outside our locus of control—are psychological issues, the destructive entanglements and lingering plots of revenge that can, with effort, be modified. Research in this area is scarce; however, the clinical experience of those in the psychological professions, myself included, supports the following suggestions:

1. *The common denominators in practically every quarrel between a former husband and wife (or between a former spouse and a successor) are underlying feelings of weakness, powerlessness, and fear.* Anger, power plays—"I'm not sending the check unless. . . . —and attempts to hurt the other person are simply vehicles to mask feelings of insecurity. A sense of one's competence as an individual rather than as half of a couple, a feeling of being able to take charge of one's own life, is almost always lacking when former spouses fail to form a working relationship. Predictably, those most crippled by hate and vengefulness are individuals who relied completely on their partner's emotional resources rather than developing their own. They have an "I am a victim of my circumstances" philosophy. This is the belief that most human unhappiness is caused by other people and outside events and that a person has virtually no control over his or her own destiny.

Blaming, retribution, self-pity, and other similar behaviors are symptomatic of this view; these are the ways we avoid accepting ultimate responsibility for our own happiness or misery. In contrast to the "I am a victim of my circumstances" philosophy —a point of view that guarantees disharmony with a former spouse—is one that expresses self-responsibility: "I have the capacity to change and find greater fulfillment." In most areas of human interaction, there are few things that cannot be accomplished. If you think, "I can't face my employer and request a raise; I can't lose weight; I can't get back into the social scene," ask yourself the following questions: If someone pointed a gun at your head and threatened to kill you if you didn't do what you say you can't do, would you do it? If your child or some other person very dear to you was in life-threatening danger and their only salvation lay in your doing what you say you can't do, would you do it? If the answer to either of these questions is yes, then ask yourself, How is it that I won't do things for my own happiness?

2. *The emotional wounds suffered in a divorce and carried into the postdivorce relationship are tied to an individual's emotional security—what he or she expects when marrying and what he or she eventually gets.* The insecure and the unrealistic suffer the most. Few of us, at least the first time around, marry out of mature love. A man may want a hostess, a mother, an accessory, a centerfold, a sister, a slave, or a tyrant. A woman may crave a father, a son, a savior, an escape from home. Continued bitterness lasting well past the formal end of a marriage signals not only emotional insecurity but the frustrations of continued—even if different—unrealized expectations: "He (she) is still not what I insist he (she) should be!" A more realistic appraisal is long past due and is likely to be facilitated with the aid of a competent psychotherapist.

3. *The most humanistic and perhaps most difficult task for adults is to refrain from damaging the children's view of their caretaker.* The children should not be unduly biased—particularly toward an absent parent—so that they can continue to relate satisfactorily to this parent until they are old enough to make their own uncoerced judgment. Children can understand an adult not liking another adult for specific reasons; but it should be made clear that this is only an opinion and that it need not influence their feelings: "People can have disagreements, just as you have disagreements with your friends. This does not mean that one of the people is *bad*—just that they have differences."

4. *Although restraint may be agonizing at times, it is unwise for the visiting parent to continue in the role of full-time disciplinarian.* Disciplinary action should be limited to those events occurring during a visit. If the children are fighting with each other, for example, the parent will comment, "Please don't fight with each other. If you have a gripe, talk it over or come to me with it. I don't like to see you hurting each other." The disciplinary action is confined to what the parent actually witnesses, in contrast to, "You kids are always fighting, I am going to instruct your mother to punish you for this. And another

thing, are you two still turning on the damn TV when you come home and leaving your homework for the morning? If so, that's going to add to your punishment!" Making demands of the children and expecting a follow-up by the custodial parent practically guarantees conflict.

5. *If a noncustodial parent does not visit the child regularly or consistently becomes involved in abrasive interactions with the child, leaving him or her distraught, it is psychologically preferable for the visits to be discontinued for a time.* Often the parent is visiting out of obligation, and after an initial defensiveness ("Are you saying I'm not a good parent!"), he or she will feel less guilty and actually be relieved by this suggestion. Perhaps at some future, less chaotic time, both parent and child can ease back into each other's life on better terms.

6. *Disputes over children are almost inevitable.* Separate relationships with the children are bound to produce conflicts of interest, quite apart from a formerly married couple's malevolence toward each other. For the children's sake, it is important that the differences be managed without stirring old resentments and allowing them to influence parenting policy. Failing this, it might be useful if separated parents bring issues regarding the children to arbitration of some sort, perhaps by a neutral professional such as a child psychologist they both trust. Each might submit opinions and the children's desires, if they are evident, and be willing to agree to the professional's judgment regarding the best interests of the child.

These, then, are some suggestions and guidelines that, if followed, can help quiet disturbing feelings and yield a nearly neutral attitude toward an ex-spouse. An essentially neutral attitude—where bitterness and fear have either vanished or are held within manageable bounds—not only brings relief for the adults involved, but also frees them to consider the welfare of their children. In some people, neutrality can even develop into a friendship. Through familiarity and a common bond with the person who was so much a part of one's life, and knowing that day-to-day friction no longer exists, a gradual friendliness begins to emerge. A woman executive, divorced four years and now remarried, reports:

"Paul, my former husband, and I see a great deal of each other and we are quite friendly. In some ways, we may even be more honest and warm than when we were married. Not having the day-to-day grind helps. We see each other or call to plan things concerning the children about once or twice a week. Politics, interesting things that have occurred, gossip about mutual friends, are also part of our conversation. Occasionally, once a month or so, the four of us, Paul and his wife and my husband, Frank, and I, have a drink together. It is always pleasant, and friendly—after all, we have nothing against each other."

This kind of friendliness, where ex-mates interact with each other's new families socially, is relatively rare. More often, if formerly married couples become friendly, it is characterized by an exchange of holiday greetings, a feeling of good will, sympathetic interest, and so on. These people are no longer directed by a worn-out script of the past but they desire to keep it in perspective; they do not wish to socialize, but they are not uncomfortable with each other. Considering the darker alternatives—hate, guilt, and fear—one need not ask for more.

# 4. A New Commitment: Preparing for Remarriage

## When Someone's Waiting

Occasionally, a marriage is broken by an affair or, as is more common, an affair rather than being the primary cause of divorce acts as a catalyst in the destruction of an unsatisfactory marriage. In either case, the usual recovery process following a dissolved marriage is diverted; instead of despair, the lovers may experience elation as they fantasize uniting in a bond that transcends the original unhappy marriage. They hope to sanctify their illicit transgression, the extramarital affair, through a new marriage. This is the idealized version. In actual life, it is a rarity. In most instances when a marriage terminates and "someone is waiting," the planned remarriage does not take place.

In my book *The Other Man, The Other Woman,* I discussed several reasons why many lovers do not marry after a divorce frees them to do so. For one thing, an affair resembles courtship, and divorce alters this. During the affair, lovers limit themselves to a narrow behavioral and social repertoire aimed at pleasing each other. Often this repertoire consists of precisely the kind of behavior lacking at home. In addition, there is the excitement of "lovers against the world"—the clandestine adventure includes secret trips, sojourns at hotels under false names, and so on. Their emotional investment in these risks convinces the lovers that the affair is the high point of their lives. With the divorce, the drama calms down, and while the strains of secrecy and jealousy are removed, new ones are introduced. For example, a lover may become suddenly apprehensive after being exposed to some unfamiliar and unpalatable divorce-battle behavior—his depleted finances, her ugly emotional outbursts, vindictiveness—all have a dampening effect on romance. Now the lovers really get to know each other and some of the revelations may be totally unexpected, if not shocking.

The experience of Harold Taylor provides an illustration of a failed love affair. After leaving his wife of eight years, he moved in with Ellen, his divorced mistress. In their two-year romance, Harold could only see Ellen for dinner once or twice a week and for an occasional weekend "business trip." Now, for the first time, they were able to be with each other without cover-ups and abrupt leave-taking. They were able to approximate more closely the role of husband and wife. It wasn't long before conflict entered the relationship. Harold had two loves. One was his electronics firm, the other—a distant second—was Ellen. It seemed to Ellen she still wasn't number one in his life.

Previously understanding and tolerant of his inability to spend more time with her, Ellen grew impatient and disturbed by the order of Harold's priorities. Now, she insisted, there was no excuse. If he worked late, she became upset. If he was tied up in his job for several days in a row, she was infuriated and openly expressed her resentment. Harold, seeing this unpleasant side of Ellen, began to have serious misgivings about marrying again; this was so despite several months of nuptial planning preceding his separation. Ellen, sensing his withdrawal and feeling frightened and betrayed, intensified her campaign of antagonism. Harold, in response, felt trapped; he began to leave for work earlier and to return home later. The cycle escalated for several weeks and the relationship eventually collapsed; the new marriage never took place.

Sometimes children complicate the picture. "I'm a pretty good father with my own kids," one recently separated man reported, "but when I got to know hers, I found them to be very mixed up and wild." This man, feeling guilty about leaving his own children to move in with his lover, reacted to her children with less than kindness. This only increased their feelings of disruption and resulted in their becoming even more demanding. Their mother was caught in the middle. At times, she sided with him and agreed that "the children needed discipline," while on other occasions, she demanded he be more tolerant of their behavior. Though she felt compelled to try to keep the children in line ("If they don't behave, he'll leave"), she hated herself for being cruel to them. Despite her strenuous effort to maintain a balance between her children's needs and her lover's patience, she failed. After four months he left.

Seeing the "darker" side of a lover—expecting more and receiving less, particularly under the duress of a divorce battle—can destroy plans for a new commitment immediately succeeding an old one. Even under more harmonious circumstances—where neither child problems nor budding ambition interfere—some people, once freed, may feel reluctant to commit themselves again. Sometimes the apprehension is actually sound judgment. An individual may realize a need to grow up, to develop and test his or her new sense of independence. In these instances, a constant companion can become an obstacle to progress.

"I met Philip at a party given by a mutual business acquaintance at the beach. We spent the fall and winter getting to know each other, a time I will cherish as the most unambiguously wonderful of my life. I found Philip to be a brilliant and dynamic man—everything my husband wasn't. After a long, exciting winter, we decided we wanted to try living together. He was single. I was involved in a stale, dispassionate marriage. There were no children. When I told my husband of my plans to move in with Philip, his protests, predictably, were mild. His strongest statement reinforced my plans: 'Well, I can't stop you if that's what you really want!' At least he could have put up a fight!

"I found living with Philip much better than living with my husband—at least he was alive! But I had a nagging sense of uneasiness. Once I was free, getting tied down again didn't appeal to me. Philip wanted very much to get married when the divorce came through, but I didn't want that. I was feeling pressured by him. I wanted to go out, meet new people, other men. I hadn't really explored standing on my own two feet, being on my own. First there was my husband—we were married very young—then there was Philip. I felt so closed in, so pressured to make the right choice—Philip would not see me if I decided to see other men. At one point I felt my whole world collapsing and I briefly considered suicide. My fantasy of suicide was actually useful to me. If I could be so disturbed about committing myself to another relationship, I knew something important was brewing within me. In a conversation with a dear friend I realized for the first time how powerful my desire for independence was. Masked by my marriage, and then by my relationship with Philip, was a very strong need to be my own person. The choice became to face life by myself for a while or spend the rest of my days in regret. I decided to choose myself. Philip and I split up and only see each other occasionally now."

When a romantic involvement that contributes to the breakup of a marriage by its promise of a fresh start fails to materialize, is there anything to be gleaned from the experience? Yes and no. Some people, particularly the chronically insecure, the highly guarded and defensive who disallow intimacy in their lives, learn little. For them, the new relationship is likely to amount to little more than self-torture. Their wounds and the wounds of those involved with them may serve to remind them that a new attachment, remarriage, does not in itself alter personal problems. Living happily with another person requires living happily with oneself. For others, the dissolution of the romance is not all pain and loss. Conversations held some time after the expiration of both the marriage and the competing affair attest to this.

From Harold Taylor:

"For years I really wanted to be out of my marriage and I wasn't able to do it. Cutting loose was torturous. There was lots of guilt to cope with. When Ellen came along and we had this wild affair, things seemed great. She provided the push for me to get out. Sadly, I found that my relationship with Ellen, after a time, began to take on the same characteristics as my marriage. This time, though, I was aware of it and put a stop to it before our differences destroyed whatever friendship remained. It was rough, but in addition to black-and-blueing our souls, both Ellen and I gained some widsom. Work is my number-one passion and I realize that very few women are going to be willing to compete with my almost exclusive devotion to business. My wife and I fought about this; Ellen and I became embroiled in the same issue. In both instances, I thought they were being unfair. But it was equally unfair of me to demand that they agree with my priorities and restructure their own wants. Neither they nor I would settle for less. We were all attempting to achieve happiness in our own way, no one was at fault. Realizing this, I am relating better to my ex-wife than ever before. Ellen and I have also become friendlier. But I'm not ready for a marriage commitment. It's too stifling—maybe someday, but not now."

And this from the woman seeking independence:

"A friend of mine, a girl I've known since I was five, got married around the same time I did. I look at her and I can see myself a few months back. The same pattern—married young, went from daddy to husband. Only I went from daddy to husband to lover. It was just too much. After both my marriage and my affair dissolved, I was at my friend's house one night. I got stoned and started shooting my mouth off about the frustrations of my marriage and about how I fell into one dependency after another. Since then, I told her, I've learned a lot of things on my own even if the learning has been a pretty lonely business. I described how I have a renewed confidence in my personal effectiveness, how I no longer live with the fear of being left by some man, how I have regained the ability to think, to imagine, to feel. Being completely on my own was the only way I could have grasped these things. I had to struggle alone in order to attain a sense of independence. Emotionally, I am stronger for the experience. My relationship with men has improved. I no longer feel like clinging and there's less game playing. I can enjoy a relationship with a man without having to be constantly on guard—that nagging voice in my head: 'What does he think of me? How am I doing? Will he ask me out again?' I've served a much needed apprenticeship with myself. One of these days marriage may even start to look good again.

"Six months after I discussed this whole thing with my friend, she called to tell me she's beginning the same routine—leaving her husband—and I feel partly responsible. I'm almost sorry I said so much. But I survived and profited enormously. My husband and my lover didn't do too badly either. They both prospered and seem happier. If my friend struggles wisely and courageously, she, too, can grow from the experience and may find her relationship with her husband or someone new to be much less neurotic and much more enriching."

But what of the extramarital romances that do evolve into marriage, how do they fare? Although the available evidence is scanty, estimates among professionals, including my own informal survey, indicate that about half work out and half either fail or are characterized as unhappy by one or both partners—a prognosis somewhat less promising than that for second marriages in general. It is likely that the factors involved in these unhappy unions include not unusual neuroses, but guilt toward the rejected marital partner, which is directed toward the present mate; important differences in interests and habits that went undetected during the affair but are expressed in the marriage; the loss of excitement that the clandestine nature of the affair provided.

Do lovers who have struggled long to possess each other live happily ever after? Sometimes yes and happily. More often not —or yes, but unhappily. Influenced by passion and consumed by the contrast between a burdensome, ailing marriage and a fresh start, the recently divorced would be wise to stop, think, and date. Going from one marriage immediately into another impedes the course of recovery, an important passage for most who have suffered a failed marriage as "rejected" or "rejector." Living alone for a time, or at the very least experimenting with a trial living-together arrangement, improves the odds for success the second time around.

## Living-Together Arrangements

Both men and women who seek a new attachment become increasingly aware of the diversity of "serious" relationships. There are factors of duration and intensity to consider, as well as practical issues such as shared households and intermeshed parenting roles. Stripped to their basics, though, committed relationships assume one of three forms: marriage, "going with someone," and living-together arrangements. The differences among these forms is in their assumed obligations—"going together" implies sexual exclusivity, living together adds to this an agreement to combine living routines, and marriage has the implication of permanence. Living-together arrangements, then, are the midpoint between the least restrictive (going with someone) and the most complex (marriage).

The current prevalence of living-together arrangements is a measure of our society's changing attitudes. Although cohabitation between the unmarried has always existed in American communities, in the past it was limited to the rich and those to whom established morality did not matter, and to the poor, who were considered to live outside the conventional boundaries. Today middle-class couples in increasing numbers are adopting this option. In the last decade, the U.S. Census Bureau reports that living-together arrangements have more than doubled. Close to two million people acknowledge living with someone without marriage; this is almost certainly a gross underestimation of the actual number since, as with any marginally accepted practice, many more people are likely to be involved than appear in formal statistical tabulations. Whether they are acknowledged openly or kept private, living-together arrangements are undeniably no longer limited to "antiestablishment" types; they have entered the mainstream of middle-class American life.

Kathy, a forty-three-year-old executive secretary divorced three years ago, affirms the change in attitude that many of the formerly married have experienced:

"Several months ago my nineteen-year-old daughter Lynn talked to me about getting married. She had been going with Eliot for about eight months and was sort of asking my permission—or, at least, my opinion—about marrying him. Not too long ago, maybe four or five years back, I would have been pleasantly taken with Lynn's plans and given her my unqualified blessings. I didn't have that reaction at all. Instead I asked a whole lot of questions: What about your plans to gain some marketable skills? How well do you really know Eliot? How prepared is he to assume the responsibilities of a husband? Why have you decided to marry at this time rather than waiting a year of two? Lynn's standard answer to all these probes was the same: 'But, Mom, we love each other!' To me, as unromantic as this seems, an answer like that is too limited. Marriage requires much more. I felt Lynn could be setting the stage either for an unhappy marriage or a divorce. I then suggested that she and Eliot try living together as a means to get to know each other better—as a way of simulating the marriage situation without the full commitment.

"My suggestion sort of stunned Lynn for a moment. She was a bit shocked that I would condone, no less promote, living together without the benefit of marriage. My attitude, although surprising to Lynn, was very natural and comfortable to me. As I look back on my own marriage, I can see that the wisest thing I could have done was to have lived with my husband and postponed having children. It probably would have meant finding out that we were ill suited, and possibly it would have saved both of us from twenty years of unhappy marriage. At the very least, it would have prepared us for the pressures and responsibilities of marriage. Instead, after six months of dating a guy who was enormously attractive, I jumped right into marriage and motherhood. I intend to marry again, but before I do, as I explained to Lynn, I know I will want to live with that person first. As far as I'm concerned, it is a necessary transition. The wider acceptance of this practice is something to praise rather than put down. It demonstrates a greater respect and awareness regarding the seriousness of the marriage commitment."

More and more people are coming to regard living-together arrangements as a laboratory in which new ways of relating can be put into practice. The very nature of the closeness allows a couple to provide each other with feedback so that they may recognize and modify relationship-defeating behaviors. Living together can provide the permissive, nonpressured kind of atmosphere needed to help sort out mixed feelings, to come to terms with unrealistic expectations, and to know and become known by another person on more intimate terms. If approached with awareness, it can broaden a person's education no matter whether the relationship is continued, dissolved, or is an interlude before remarriage.

Simply moving in with another person ensures none of these benefits automatically. Whether it be in marriage or a less formal commitment, the experience of living with another person requires effort and realistic expectations. Some people seem to drift into such relationships casually, without extensive discussion. Though the apparent casualness may be only a device by which the man and woman retain emotional options despite the appearance of commitment, often it is based on convenience. The decision may be precipitated by a need to move from a previous residence, or regarded as an easy way to be "taken care of," or seen as an economic measure or a way to avoid loneliness. None of these factors is in itself unusual or a warning

# A New Commitment

of trouble ahead. Practically every living-together arrangement (and every marriage) contains elements of convenience. However, when the primary motive for living together is convenience or emotional shelter—to avoid developing one's inner resources—the benefits derived are likely to be quite limited. A living-together arrangement can provide a testing ground for remarriage if the participants actively work at the relationship, rather than waiting passively, as many married couples do, for it to prosper by itself.

Jennifer Bates and Allen Lang, both divorced, decided to live together after having known each other for over a year. Their report, after six months of cohabitation, illustrates the creative use of this option as a bridge to a new commitment. Jennifer reveals:

"We wanted something more than our dating relationship was affording us. I—both of us—looked forward to being able to share our lives. Despite high hopes, though, there were many fears and uncertainties: Would the realities of stronger obligations to each other crush the friendship we had achieved? There really was no way to tell until we took the risk. The only thing we were sure of was that we enjoyed each other's company immensely and that we were not yet prepared to marry. Neither of us trusted ourselves enough to say with finality that we could tolerate the other's idiosyncrasies and work out differences between us satisfactorily. We just did not have enough of that kind of experience with each other. Living together, we hoped, would give us that experience. Several very basic guidelines were established: We agreed the relationship would be monogamous; it would have no time limit nor would it necessarily result in marriage; and, since both of us worked, we agreed to share household tasks equally.

"After about three months I had fallen into a familiar trap. I was playing the compliant little girl, taking Allen's lead even when it conflicted with what I really wanted. Whether it was going out with his friends, listening to his choice of music, or the evening's meal, it seemed I was always deferring to his preference. I would always go along with things like a nice little girl. Isn't that how you keep a man's love? At least that's what I grew up believing—foolishly. Because of my conflict about this issue, there was a great deal of resentment in me and a mounting tension between us. Remembering the pain of my marriage helped me work up the courage to discuss things with Allen. I could not allow myself to get into another relationship and maintain it on false premises. To my surprise, Allen was not rejecting but rather encouraged me to be more assertive. To me, being assertive was equivalent to being pushy. But, as I found out later in an assertiveness training group, it is simply communicating your wants and dislikes without unnecessarily hurting another person. Even if our relationship had not lasted, that part of my experience with Allen, where I was able for the first time to openly express myself, strengthened me enormously and was worth the risk."

From Allen:

"I don't take the issue about Jenny not asserting herself lightly. I could feel her silent resentment and it was really getting to me. My hunch is that many relationships falter because of these very kinds of things. I actually found it a relief when she told me what was bugging her. The reality was much easier to deal with than my fantasy: 'She probably dislikes me; she's bored with me; maybe I'm not doing well as a lover.' Each time I would ask, 'What's the matter?' I would get a sullen, 'Nothing.' Yet the strained smiles and the condemnatory looks said something much different. It was confusing as hell.

"After that initial breakthrough in which Jenny discussed how she felt, both of us worked on sharing our feelings—the negative ones in particular—in a manner that promoted understanding between us so that we could remedy the difficulty. We worked at *not* attacking each other. Both of us had had more than our share of attack–counterattack! Developing a more tolerant attitude, particularly when the differences were severe, was damn difficult. I think our very strong commitment to learn to live with another person—whether or not it evolved into a marriage—was our greatest asset. We were under no illusion that it was going to be easy."

Living together enabled Jennifer and Allen to move in the direction of increased involvement that eventually included marriage. For others, living together may not result in marriage but rather in a decision to separate. In these instances, the distress that follows may not be as severe as that which follows the ending of a marriage, but there is a special loneliness felt since married friends and relatives—underestimating the emotional intensity of this "informal" experience—are less likely to be empathic. Here, too, despite the hardship, there is something to be gained: If we enter a relationship with another person honestly, whether it continues or not, we are bound to learn more about ourselves, and our increased self-awareness is bound to improve our subsequent intimate relationships.

## Selective Selection: The Choice of Mate

Living-together arrangements, if viewed realistically, constitute a useful halfway station to marriage. However, because the emotional impact of marriage makes it unlike any other experience, inability to manage living together may be a reliable indication of inability to manage marriage, but success in living together does not guarantee success in marriage. Very few endeavors involving people, particularly in affairs of the heart, yield simple predictions. In the course of relationships between the sexes, the path is rocky and not well marked. Living-together arrangements can be a useful step toward clearing the path.

Another important step involves choosing a partner on a sound basis. The question of who married whom and why is of perennial interest, but only in the last half-century has it become the subject of scientific research. Throughout American history there has always been a romantic theory of mate selection, supported by poets, dramatists, and the public at large: "Love is blind" and "The best marriages are made in heaven." Social scientists, however—a group of jaundiced realists, by and large—have little faith in this pleasant myth. They insist that the probability of having a workable marriage depends on making a hard-headed assessment. If this is not done—and often it is not because neither human nature nor the Western tradition encourage us to be rational in our choice of a mate—the notion of personal responsibility, an important factor both in selecting one's mate and in making the marriage workable, is damaged.

Some psychologists, marriage counselors, and family therapists—particularly those who are Freudian in orientation—take the view that people who had an unhappy first marriage are destined to make the same mistakes and encounter the old problems again in remarriage. They support their position with the Freudian proposition that contends that childhood experiences dramatically and unalterably shape the actions of adulthood. Redirection resulting in a healthier outlook is possible only through intensive psychotherapy.

Exponents of this view state that although nearly all the previously married believe they know themselves better, have learned a lot from their past, and will be more successful in their next attempt, they are sadly mistaken. Those who were neurotically joined, the Freudians report, are condemned by the conflicts locked in the hidden recesses of their psyche to repeat in a new relationship the events of the former marriage. Adult experiences, they hold, are not potent enough to penetrate and modify the unconscious in any significant manner; hence, those who were involved in a failed first marriage are unlikely to have grown wiser in the process. "Since the neurotic is unconsciously on the lookout for his complementary neurotic type," wrote the late psychoanalyst Dr. Edmund Bergler, "the chances of finding conscious happiness in the next marriage are exactly zero.... The second, third and nth marriages are but repetitions of previous experiences."

Clearly, not everyone chooses a second marriage partner as unwisely as Dr. Bergler suggests. The majority are more exacting than they were with their first husband or wife. Some, however, choose a new mate on the basis of ready availability. They may think themselves in the grip of a special and unduplicated passion but, out of insecurity, neurotic deprivation, or overwhelming pressure from family and friends, they choose someone conveniently near who promises acceptance. Few people, of course, are willing to acknowledge their "grand passion" owes a great deal to nearness and willingness. Most prefer to believe they are being controlled by a power of love greater than themselves.

Other people choose a mate whom they consider inferior, a compromise choice dictated by their fear that they are unacceptable to the "superior" person they would prefer but don't dare aspire to. Because of the felt inequality, a marriage made on this basis soon moves into crisis.

Another basis for choice that causes every bit as much trouble is the search for "actualization." These people marry to improve themselves. They look for someone who has qualities they admire and wish they had, with the idea that this mate will complete them and allow them to leap over their deficiencies. "I want," a divorced woman once told me with hunger and wistfullness, "to find a man who is large and wise and better than me." People who choose a mate on this basis often find that after the initial attraction has subsided, they are on a downhill course.

When Alec and Marie met, they were immediately attracted to each other. Both had experienced unhappy first marriages and each seemed to provide the missing element in the other's life. They saw each other constantly for three months, felt very much in love, and married.

Alec had always considered himself an outsider. He felt awkward with people in general and was especially uncomfortable in and unwilling to play the role of the pursuing male that "the dating game" called for.

Marie handled her insecurities by becoming socially gregarious. A striking redhead of thirty-four, brisk and saucy in manner, and highly efficient as a personal secretary, she nonetheless needed constant reassurance of her lovability. Marie surrounded herself with a large network of friends and acquaintances. She felt most comfortable in a crowd. After seeking fulfillment in a score of affairs and finding it only very briefly in each, she began to feel a very strong desire to marry again.

Initially, Marie saw Alec as a man at peace with himself—a man who could stand alone, as a good listener and someone she could rely on. As for Alec, he felt Marie was the answer to his prayers. His anxieties about dating were quieted with Marie—she did most of the talking, arranged their socializing, and generally led the way into areas Alec wouldn't dare enter alone.

Alec and Marie began their relationship in a whirlwind, thinking they were beautifully matched. But their love didn't last. Because both lacked important qualities in their own personalities, they mistook the other's weakness as a strength. Each had entered the relationship with a hidden agenda. Each expected the other to supply the characteristic that he or she lacked. Within a few months the relationship began to deteriorate. Alec's basic uneasiness around people and Marie's inability to be away from others proved increasingly disruptive.

Alec withdrew further and became very critical of Marie's need for constant companionship. Marie, wanting to be at the hub of Alec's life, reacted defensively to his withdrawal by redoubling her social efforts and demanding constant reassurance —which only served to anger Alec and get her less of what she wanted. Alec became increasingly self-conscious as their relationship withered.

Marie felt trapped. She was getting less "lovability" feedback from her husband and resented his unwillingness to spend time with friends. Ashamed to continue going to parties and gatherings alone ("They are going to think Alec and I are having troubles"), Marie found herself shut off from her usual "reassurance sounds."

Two years of this escalating cycle had left Marie and Alec in a relationship where resentfulness, despair, and bitterness had replaced the original ecstasy. There was no real communication and whatever feeling they once had for each other had soured.

# A New Commitment

Shortly after the second year of marriage, they were divorced.

Marriage, as it became evident to Alec and Marie, is difficult enough even when the spouses do not have behavioral repertoires that clash or are mutually incomprehensible. When these extreme differences are built into a marriage, it is a definite handicap. Of course, there are marriages that seem to thrive despite marked differences between the spouses, but they are most unusual. In general, the degree of consonance between the value systems of the spouses is of major importance in determining marital compatibility. Although many of us are acquainted with spouses who are opposite in various ways and still have a successful marriage, the differences are generally in noncritical areas, and therefore without major significance.

Whatever their orientation, most professionals in the field concur that those considering remarriage need exposure to a wide array of human beings. Youth embraces a range of characteristics and qualities as acceptable, but maturity—and most of the formerly married are past their mid-twenties—limits the sorts of experiences and people that bring satisfaction. The number of people with whom we would want to live decreases. To find another person who shares our cherished tastes and preferences and value system is exceedingly more difficult than in youth. The process requires a refined maturity, social exposure, time, patience, and a bit of luck.

Although the psychological professions are unable to provide a ready formula for compatible mate selection, they do offer some guidelines: Before remarrying, take a careful inventory of past marital conflicts to be sure they are not directing your current behavior. If you are remarrying to prove you can be a good husband or wife despite the painful experience of a previous marriage, don't remarry yet; you are not ready. If you are remarrying to punish an ex-spouse or to prove you are lovable, you are similarly not ready for remarriage. Remarriage will not mend past wounds; indeed, if the healing has not been complete, the pressure of a new commitment is likely to result in a sharply disconcerting rupture. Those who rush into remarriage as soon as a previous marriage terminates, and even those who move at a leisurely pace but without undergoing the work of rehabilitation, are unlikely to shed whatever psychological problems or areas of ignorance remain from their previous marriage. Give yourself a chance to mourn. Look around you, at yourself and who you are. Develop a feeling of your autonomous self before taking on the responsibility of choosing a marital partner.

Ask these questions of yourself and your prospective mate: Do we have many interests in common? Do we have independent interests but tolerate each other's activities? Do we expect to develop interests in common? Or do we seem to have relatively little in common when we are not busy with social activities? If there are very few common interests, it is likely that companionship, a major reason for remarrying, will be adversely affected.

A list of practical items for discussion with a prospective spouse might include the following:

1. Why will this marriage be different from the previous one?

2. Does he/she have any hang-ups that will make an open and communicative relationship difficult?

3. Has he/she grown since the termination of the previous marriage?

4. Are we sexually and emotionally compatible?

5. What kind of people does he/she prefer? Is there compatibility in this area?

6. What are his/her views toward such important issues as parenting, religion, and money?

No matter how hard they attempt to be objective in a discussion such as this, prospective mates have a strong tendency to rationalize. A trusted third party can be helpful in keeping the dialogue on an even keel and assuring more objective conclusions. As a rule, the greater the gap between the couple on the above issues, the greater the likelihood they will have difficulty in forming a highly functional relationship.

## Remarriage Prognosis

Until the past decade, most people, including professionals in the field, tended to consider all remarriages "problematical." They took an especially disapproving view of remarriage after divorce, which they pictured in terms of quarrels and frustrations, suffering children, and self-centered spouses irresponsibly fleeing their legitimate duties. Considering the sorry state of so many intact marriages, some of the disapproval may have stemmed from envy masked as moral reprobation. Even remarriage after widowhood suggested to these critics such "unresolvable" problems as "stepchild–stepparent" hostilities resulting from the children's opposition to the remarriage of the surviving parent and their resentment that the bereaved could be so quickly consoled. This attitude also may stem from envy that bereavement had honorably released another for a venture that, for the critics, could be accomplished only by divorce, with its grim toll.

Attitudes toward remarriage are now in a process of reconstruction in our culture. Most American communities (there are notable exceptions) view remarriage with tolerance, if not complete approval. There has been a gradual increase in the amount of attention paid to the divorced and widowed and to remarriage in etiquette books and popular magazines as well as in professional journals. Gradually we are liberalizing our attitudes not only toward the dissolution of marriages but also toward the creation of second marriages.

It is evident that remarriage has increased in recent years; it is also gaining wider acceptance; but what chance is there that it will succeed? This is an issue about which experts have differing opinions. In contrast to the skeptical Freudians are a large number of professionals, myself included, who believe that personality change and emotional growth is more fluid than Freud realized. We take the position that the formerly married, if they choose, can substantially improve their judgment, emotional capacity, and self-knowledge; and that therefore they are in a position to do better in their second marriages.

What is more, many social scientists report that investigations of failed first marriages reveal not neurosis, but the normal errors and misjudgments common to the inexperienced. For example, renowned sociologist Dr. Jesse Bernard found in an extensive study of remarriage that the majority of first-marriage failures were caused by "incompatibility factors." These were marriages in which the individuals were quite normal. They simply were poorly matched. Professor Bernard concluded that for the most part, the deficiencies of these individuals consisted of inexperience. "The experiences of an unhappy first marriage," she writes, "although they may constitute a high tuition fee, may nevertheless serve as a valuable educational prerequisite to a successful second marriage."

Professor Bernard's own study, *Remarriage,* bears her out on this point. Her findings, based on ratings of over two thousand remarriages including both the divorced and widowed, were that seven-eighths of them were satisfactory to extremely satisfactory; only one-eighth were reported to be unsatisfactory or extremely unsatisfactory. Psychologist Harvey J. Locke, in an independent study, presented similar results in his book *Predicting Adjustment in Marriage.* In his survey of 146 remarriages, he found three-quarters of them to be happy or very happy, and only one out of nine unhappy or very unhappy; the remainder lay in between.

Lillian Messinger, another researcher, at the Clarke Institute of Psychiatry, provided testimony (reported in *Psychology Today's* Newsline, November 1976) with a different tone. Ms. Messinger interviewed seventy remarried couples in the first stage of a large research project on second families. She found problems aplenty—new ones that neither our culture nor previous marriages had prepared these people to handle. Most couples agreed with other married and divorced persons in ranking the partner's immaturity, sexual difficulties, and personal lack of marriage readiness as the biggest problems of their first marriages. They put children and money at the bottom of this list. But children and money were at the top of their list of difficulties in the second marriage.

As a permanent link to ex-spouses, children can squeeze parents between the roles they played in their first marriage and those they are trying to develop for their second. Messinger points out that our culture has not yet evolved traditions that provide remarried parents with a model of appropriate behavior. In addition, single-parent families can become closed systems that are hard for a new spouse to enter. Messinger found that "while couples were generally aware that remarriage meant a major personal adjustment, they very often expressed surprise at their underestimation of the emotional upheaval involved for the children, as they attempted to integrate into the new marital household, with its different lifestyle and with a different adult in an authority role."

Many partners were caught between loyalty to their own children and their desire to please a new mate. Others felt guilty for not loving their new children. Even space became a problem. In families that stayed in one partner's old house, "the new residents felt like invaders and the old residents felt displaced and resisted sharing their territory."

Financial problems frequently sprang up because of obligations left over from first marriages. Women felt guilty about the burden their children placed on their new husbands, and men felt reluctant to reveal their true financial assets. Some women kept money aside in case of another failed marriage; some men refused to revise their wills and insurance policies for the same reason. For many newly joined couples, money and financial matters thus became a sensitive issue that neither wanted to confront. This tendency of avoidance was sometimes present in other areas of potential conflict.

Reports such as Messinger's do not suggest that remarriages are destined to fail. Rather, they show that remarried couples are still vulnerable to the problems of living with another person, that making two families into one involves unanticipated complexities. Marriage, it is evident, is not a foolproof relationship either the first or the second time.

This brings us to a related question: How enduring are second marriages? Dr. Paul Glick, senior demographer at the U.S. Census Bureau, concluded from data compiled through 1976 that in addition to the 36 percent of first marriages that end in divorce (a little over one in three), 38 percent of second marriages also dissolve. Dr. Glick conjectures that one reason many second marriages fail is that people who have already been through one divorce do not hesitate to divorce again, if necessary. They are less tolerant of living unhappily.

Bernice and Morton Hunt, themselves remarried, also offer a positive interpretation of the Census Bureau's findings in their book *The Divorce Experience:*

Even though the success of second marriages is so close to that of first marriages, a truer measure of their success is seen in the comparison of the survival rates of the first and second marriages of the same people. *Obviously, zero per cent of those who were divorced the first time remained happy enough to stay in the marriage, but 62 per cent of those people will stay married the second time.* When we compare the success of those who remarry to their success the first time, the result is a ringing affirmation of the divorce experience.

Obviously, remarriage is not all good or all bad; it is, like any other personal relationship, some of each. Many individuals benefit from remarriage, others do not. And 62 percent success isn't at all bad considering that second marriages may be subject to formidable obstacles: The sniping of ex-spouses; the complications introduced by children of earlier marriages; and the reluctance of both relatives and friends to accept what they may think of as a replacement spouse. In fact, the degree of success the remarried have achieved is remarkable. It is quite likely that as we become more informed of the remarriage process and as our society's acceptance of this practice grows, second marriages will do even better.

# The Making of a Stepchild 5

## The Loss

It is no exaggeration to say that the center of a child's world is his family. The family determines social relations, shapes adaptive habits, and influences personal well-being. When this mainstay is shattered, the youngster's sense of self and security is threatened. Separation anxiety is a powerful force that looms threateningly at the edge of every child's life. The signs of distress to even temporary absence—a parent's hospitalization, extended trips away from home, or a child's first day at school—are familiar to most parents. Among the most common are painful cries of protest, moodiness, withdrawals, and behavioral disturbances.

Jeremy, a seven-year-old boy whose parents have recently separated, has been suffering from nightmares and a variety of fears. Nonetheless, he puts up a bold front; several of the neighborhood children no longer want to play with him because of his aggressiveness. In one psychotherapy session, he seemed particularly upset; when asked what was troubling him, he remained silent. A few minutes later he picked up some toys, his "little people," and became engrossed in a highly emotional drama. The man and woman dolls were at war. They were shooting at each other with their miniature army tanks, jet fighters, and machine guns. It wasn't long before the armed camps of these two "enemies," the man and the woman, were sharply divided. Each violently attacked and hurled missiles at the other.

Soon another "little person" was introduced into the drama. This, Jeremy explained, was a child who was lost and wandered into the war zone. "When the big people spotted him," Jeremy continued, "they fought over whose side he would be on." They each started to pull at him, each demanded he be on their side. All this was accompanied by angry screams from the "big people" and sounds of frightful whimpering by the "little person."

"Suddenly there's a gigantic explosion!" Jeremy screamed. "A big bomb lands right in the middle of the war zone, right between the man and the woman." Jeremy went on to describe how the bomb resulted in an enormous crater that left the man and woman so far away that they couldn't see each other again. Holding the miniature figures in his small hands and stretching his arms to keep them as far apart as he could, Jeremy paused, then finished his very personal enactment with this remark: "And the little boy who was lost fell down and down, deep into the hole between the man and the woman."

The fear that Jeremy so powerfully expressed through his play is provoked by his sense that his world is crumbling; that the people who take care of him will hurt each other or abandon him and that he will not survive this horrible ordeal. This possibility haunts most children and is, on occasion, realized through the actual loss of a parent. The combination of factors that determine how children will react to the loss of a parent are infinite; it is an impossibly imprecise area. Among the major variables are these: the point in the child's development at which the loss occurs; whether it is the mother or father who is lost; and whether the severed relationship is the result of death or divorce.

Most parents, and stepchildren themselves in retrospect,

agree that pubescence and adolescence are probably the worst times to lose a parent; it is a particularly stormy period to adjust to remarriage. Very young and near-adult children tend to make easier adjustments. This may be because the adolescent and pubescent experience a protracted mourning process in contrast to the younger or older child. Some adolescents postpone their mourning by marrying. In effect, they replace the lost parent with a spouse of their own, often to the bewilderment, and relief, of both parent and stepparent. For many adolescents, the particularly long duration of mourning is likely a byproduct of the defensive posture characteristic of children in the age range twelve–sixteen: excessive indifference, reserve, and a facade of toughness. Trauma does not easily penetrate this protective armor; for it to be comprehended, digested into the psychological system, and accepted requires a variant, but usually lengthy, passage of time.

Of course, there is no "best age" at which to lose a parent. The dissolution of a marriage and a subsequent remarriage are practically always problematic from infancy through adolescence. Interestingly, many stepparents believe it is easier to deal with an older stepchild, arguing that he will soon be out of the house and on his own. A younger child may adjust to a parent's remarriage more quickly and easily, but he will also require more parenting for a longer period of time.

Since the mother is the one who is usually primarily responsible for the child's needs during a large part of the day, her loss is often more disruptive to a child than the loss of a father. An emotional realignment begins when the powerful bond with mother is rocked. At first, feelings are denied; the finality that mother is gone—either through death or divorce—takes children a long time to comprehend. The loss is a devastating blow, and children work mightily to suppress this fact in an effort to quiet their unrest. When the loss is acknowledged, there is a surge of anger, hurt, and fear: Mother has betrayed the child. On whom can he depend? The sex of the child enters here as another variable. A boy who loses his mother may not endure the guilty torture that his sister does, if she, locked in a cycle of jealousy, rivalry, and negativism with her mother, had been wishing her ill-will. Both male and female children at this difficult point in their lives turn to their father. They rely on him more than ever to help them accept their mother's departure, and for protection.

While coming to terms with the parting of a mother is a grievous process for children, the loss of this parent is less frequent. The great majority of stepchildren suffer the loss of a father; premature death and custody laws are biased against men. Thus men who wed a previously married woman—whether widow or divorcée—live with her children unless she is among the minority of women who have chosen or have been forced to relinquish custody of their children. Although it is the more common occurrence, losing a father is no easy matter.

One of the more frequent effects of a father's absence has to do with sex roles. Boys who are fatherless or who see their fathers only irregularly are at an obvious disadvantage. Not having a male around to provide a model, they are likely to have a blurred picture of what masculine behavior entails. Societal pressure to conform to strict sex-role behavior often leads them to the extremes; in their uncertainty about masculinity, they overreact and become hyperaggressive. Indeed, the research evidence indicates this confusion lies behind the destructive behavior of a sizable number of delinquent boys who have suffered the absence of a father. A father surrogate in the form of an older brother or other male who has regular contact with the child and provides a positive image can serve as an antidote to aggressive overreaction.

For the daughter, the effect of a father's absence is likely to take a different direction. Her loss is the opportunity to continue relating to a man in whom she has a heavy emotional investment. Mother often is seen as the wicked witch who sent Daddy away; the daughter will frequently direct her anger at her mother, and multiply it a few times. The expression of her anger may be direct and forceful; more frequently, it is more passive than in her male counterpart. Overeating, slipping school grades, and deliberate but masked provocations are common. One girl, for example, aware of her divorced mother's concern for what the neighbors thought, would lure her mother into loud, revealing arguments on the front lawn.

Most authorities believe that the way the previous marriage ended is an important determinant of the child's emotional reaction and, equally, his eventual relationship to a stepparent. The question often asked is which is harder to accept, a loss through death or divorce? The response of stepfamily members is invariably mixed. Stepparents by divorce, of course, report that stepparenting through death is easier—"If only the ex-spouse were dead," they plead, "and I had the kids all to myself, then I could gain their loyalty." The widowed are convinced otherwise—"The idealization of the dead is so strong I could never measure up," they argue.

Children who have experienced a divorce in their family often feel a sense of betrayal that at some point radiates into anger. Their parents' failure to resolve disagreements is viewed as "giving up"—an unacceptable course to the security-oriented child. Even after the final divorce decree it is not uncommon for children to persist in trying to reunite their parents. Some children become so caught up in the reconciliation process that they feel guilty and blame themselves if it fails. They feel *they* should have tried harder to stop the divorce. The child's sense of being to blame and his consequent doubts as to his lovability combine with a confusing resentment toward his parents to unleash a disorienting turmoil.

When a parent dies, underneath the surface emotion there is a tiny but piercing doubt in the child—"Did Mommy (Daddy) really love me? If I was really cherished, why would Mommy (Daddy) leave me?" Children are likely to idealize the dead parent, making him or her into an omnipotent image—"Daddy (Mommy) always had time for me; Daddy (Mommy) never was grumpy."

There is quite an opposite tendency when divorce has been the means of exit. Usually, there is a protracted period of anger, snarling, weeping, and threatening between parents before the decision to divorce is made. Children cannot help but bear witness to great quantities of marital conflict in these instances. Even in the most civilized divorces, children become involved. Angry grief and shattered egos hardly encourage loving, kind behavior. Often parents have vicious, damaging battles in front of the children; each tries to win the children's loyalty by emphasizing the defects of the other. Each is out to prove the badness of the other and thereby destroy the other's credibility. This ugliness undermines the children's respect for their parents and shatters their belief that they will always be safe. How can they feel secure when the people who were their guides through adversity are tearing each other apart? Some youngsters are shaken to their core and become unsure of themselves. They may feel significantly less capable—they are the crew members of a sinking ship. Commonly, children conclude that if their parents failed to maintain a viable family, they, too, will fail when they grow up.

Which is harder to accept, a loss through death or divorce? The divorced and widowed respond with obvious bias. In actuality, the picture is blurred; life is not neat. There are, as Brenda Maddox reports in *The Half-Parent,* a great many divorced parents who might as well be dead for all the involvement they have with their children, and there are a great many parents taken by death who would have divorced had they remained alive. The child who lost a parent through death may have experienced the discord and dissension attributed to the divorced. The divorced, as all parents will acknowledge, do not have an option on discord.

Idealization of a deceased parent can be a drawback as well as a benefit. It is a drawback when used as protection by the child —"No one else can measure up to my Mother (Father), so no one else is worth loving." It is a benefit if the ideal of the lost parent enlarges the child's receptivity toward a replacement— "Mother (Father) was good to me and loved me, so other women (men) can be good to me and love me."

## Between Marriages

The family is a small but complicated organization. Its members have intertwining ties. When a parent departs, there is a shift or reordering among the remaining members. The nature of the change that occurs is likely to rub off on the children and influence the process of adjustment to a parent's remarriage.

Consider the experience of Phyllis, a bright, studious youngster whose father died suddenly three years ago when she was twelve. Naomi, Phyllis's mother, is an unstable child-woman who was emotionally propped up by a dominant husband. She was treated as a second daughter. Naomi is an occasional actress, who more often than not appears for auditions in an alcoholic stupor. Phyllis's sense of assault on herself and her world was expressed not only by words but also by frequent unbearable tension in her head, a severe loss of appetite, inability to concentrate in school, and occasional relief in promiscuity.

"I am afraid about all the trouble my mother is having. The only time I'm happy is when I'm asleep—but I wake up at night. I'm having all these horrible dreams. I used to pour my mother's liquor down the sink, but she would just get mad at that and get some more. I didn't think it would come to this. Maybe she is just a thirty-nine-year-old baby, but she's wonderful too. She can be really fantastic. She is beautiful, sparkling, charming, and smart, and my friends really like her. She can be lovable and very warm.

"But I can't count on her. She acts so helpless at times—out of control. I'm confused. Whenever I try to get close or ask her for advice, she seems as if she wants me to take care of *her*. I wish I could, but I can't. No one wants to see how it is with *me*. I can be at the point of suicide and no one would want to see it. Once my aunt tried to tell me how terrific I am, that I'm really fantastic, but I was trying to tell her I felt like jumping off a bridge. She pretended that everything was well and went on to tell me that everyone feels 'blue' at times."

Phyllis's dilemma is caused by a parent who feels unusually inadequate and uncertain about how to cope. Losing a marital partner practically always provokes a degree of insecurity, though usually far less extreme than in this case. Children quickly detect this and become uncertain about themselves—frequently they mirror a parent's reaction. They may, in desperation, rely more heavily on the remaining parent and expect to reap undivided attention. The lone parent is likely to think the walls are closing in and to feel pressured beyond endurance. Feeling burdened in proportion to the children's distress, the parent will often react with a counterdemand: "I need you to support and comfort me." Unlike the child's plea for help, the parent's demand for psychological support is likely to be indirect. For example, the parent may draw unusually close to the children in an apparently nurturant stance, but in so doing deliver the underlying message: "You must keep very close to me; I need you to prop me up." Not only does this type of entanglement slow the maturing process of the children, but when a new mate comes into the parent's life, the child is further confused: "Will Mother (Father) still love me? Where are my loyalties?"

Another variation demonstrated by the insecure parent, and cited by psychologists Seymour and Rhoda Fisher in their book *What We Really Know about Child Rearing,* is the mother who has severed the relationship with her husband but who in her loneliness after the divorce begins to miss him. If she has a son, Seymour and Rhoda Fisher note, "she may use him as a substitute to take the place of her former husband." She may expect him to assume some of the father's previous responsibilities, which in itself is not damaging, but she may also impose upon him for emotional intimacy—a psychological pressure that is likely to trouble him. Along with the demand to be "a substitute for Daddy" is the demand that he function as a target for anger meant for "Daddy." So the youngster finds himself simultaneously tugged toward Mother and told he is bad—"You act just like your father." This is another instance in which confusion is likely to exaggerate the normally mixed feelings that are provoked in a child upon a parent's remarriage.

The heightened anxiety and insecurity a parent experiences at the loss of a mate frequently affects disciplinary practices. Parents typically support each other on most disciplinary practices; this makes enforcing standards in the face of a child's resistance much easier. Parents who are left alone are likely to be particularly uncertain in this area. Some become less firm and consistent in administering discipline. They give in to their children's every whim either because they feel guilty (in the case of the parent who leaves) or because they want the child's affection (in the case of the parent who stays). The tendency in both instances is to smooth over any feelings of anger and deprivation the child may be experiencing. This serves no one well. It will likely corrupt the children, make it impossible to live with them, and probably create conflict when the hope for a new marital partner is realized.

Some parents take an opposite tack and become harsh. Many adolescent boys and girls, especially those living with a mother, have very strong negative feelings about being overcontrolled. Their feelings—stronger than those of their counterparts in intact families—reflect the actions of a parent who is overreacting in order to convey a strong message: "Don't think that just because I am alone I am no longer the boss; I'm still very much in charge." Children in this circumstance are usually tempted to fight back. They refuse to follow "all those rules," and the mother or father reacts by imposing still stricter constraints and by becoming further entrenched in an authoritarian stance.

Harshness, just as much as inconsistent and lax discipline, has severe consequences. Many children, angry at being treated unfairly, work at sabotaging their parent's remarriage efforts. They sense remarriage is an important goal and seek to "balance the books" for unjust treatment. Others continue angrily to defy their parent as if to prove they have individuality—"Just as it is important that you feel in control, I feel it is important that you realize I am not a puppetlike extension of you."

One of the most common occurrences in a broken family is a reshuffling of family roles. Sometimes a child who has been the favorite may abruptly be pushed aside because the remaining parent chooses to confer this special status on one of the other children. Usually children find these role changes confusing and stressful. Linda, eighteen, had such an experience. She found herself cast in the role of "Blessed Child." She comments on what it was like for her:

"My mother and father both made me their favorite. That was strange to me. Up until the time they separated—I was fifteen then—they didn't even seem to notice me. Jerry, my younger brother, seemed to get all the attention. All of a sudden, they both turned to me. I was the young woman; I was the confidante. I felt like God's special gift to the world. Dad, up to his ears in debt, shelled out for a brand new car for me when I turned seventeen. All I had to do was mention that I passed my driving course, and there it was, two weeks later, in front of the house. My mother couldn't top that one; I knew she was fuming. Here she was still wearing her threadbare coat for another winter because money was tight, and my father comes up with this outrageous gift.

"You would think I was jumping for joy about this whole thing. I wasn't. I had mixed feelings. I liked the attention and played into it, but I was wary. I knew my elevated status rested on a whim—my father's. The situation was apt to change any day. I didn't believe I was his favorite; he was using me to cleanse his own conscience, to make up for past injustices, to get back at my mother, or something. My mother, rather than continuing to compete with my father—which she couldn't win at—began to get very hard on me, as if to offset my father's 'partiality.' I was also rebounding off this thing. My relationship with my brother—which had always been good—was going downhill. I was picking fights with him so that we didn't spend time together; I was uncomfortable as the favored one. Even though I wasn't really favored, I felt guilty around Jerry. He was being left out and was upset a lot of the time."

In contrast to Linda's experience, but with similar consequences, a child may find that when the marriage dissolves, his parents compete to find fault with him (the "fault" allegedly "inherited" from the other spouse). This strategy is a favorite way of getting at the partner who is more sensitive to the child's needs—which is one reason why it is dangerous in an emotionally embroiled divorce for a child to be a favorite of one parent. It invites misuse of the child as a weapon. In extreme situations, it may even result in physical cruelties. In any case, the child is apt to suffer emotionally either through overindulgence of his whims or severe deprivation. The conclusion is likely to be the child's loss of respect for the parents and a perpetuation of infantile behavior. Moreover, the child's ability to adjust well to a parent's remarriage will be substantially diminished.

Still another crucial matter concerns the nature of outside contact sought by the remaining spouse. At some point, a parent is bound to turn to social activities in which potential new sex partners and potential new spouses can be encountered. Dating begins. Some children, particularly if their parent's date is friendly and competent with them, will respond warmly and enthusiastically. They may even exert pressure for more exposure to the potential parent/companion. In many instances, though, the match does not come about regardless of the children's desires, and they are left disappointed—maybe even heartbroken.

Virginia Harris, a gentle, noncompetitive person employed part time teaching school, has been single four years. Her ten-year-old son, Donald, is particularly attached to Larry, her steady companion. Tonight at dinner, Ms. Harris is faced with a disturbing task. She will have to tell Donald that Larry will not be around anymore; the relationship has been waning for months and has finally terminated. What Virginia Harris dreads most at this time is not her future—she will be all right—but Donald's disappointment and hurt, the look she expects to see in his eyes. There have been other men she saw steadily who then dropped out of sight. Each time, it was upsetting to Donald.

Donald, as it turned out, was resilient and was only temporarily dismayed by his disappointment. Many children, desirous of a second parent, also continue to be receptive in spite of shattered hopes. The reactions of other children, however, are far less tolerant and can be quite disconcerting—especially since they have a way of delaying them until the worst possible moment. Marjorie, a widow who has just started dating, explains: "Although I told Jason, my four-year-old son, about my plans to spend time with male friends and thought he accepted the idea, just as we were about to leave, he panicked and fired a barrage of questions—'Can I come? Is he going to stay here? Are you coming back?' " Last minute rebellions need not assume a question-answer format; sometimes they are more dramatically staged. Small children may cry, fight with their siblings, or become instantly in dire need of undivided attention. Older ones may suddenly remember the book report that required parental consultation; they may attempt to destroy any trace of romantic atmosphere by acting brazen, aloof, or rude toward the potential competitor for Mother's or Father's attention. And sometimes it works; it is no coincidence that after the children are introduced, some potential love affairs die unborn.

To children, ever alert to change, dating presents the chilling possibility that a new parent can be formally added through remarriage. Many children are vividly affected by this because they sense that things are transitory—"If a parent can be removed and a stranger brought in to join the family, the future is not predictable." There is a recurring question: "Will my Mother (Father) still be close to me or will this 'new person' become a wedge between us?" Jealousy and the fear of change occupy a central position. Coping with these feelings toward remarriage—which can range from vague and only mildly nagging doubts to overwhelming panic—and the flow of emotion evoked in direct response to the presence of the stepparent is the next task of the stepchild.

## Remarriage

Jeffrey is a sophomore in college. He was six when his father died and nine when his mother remarried. Although his intellect immediately comprehended the change, Jeffrey's emotions required more time; it took him seven years to readjust to the new alliance. Until he was sixteen, he had been rebellious, unsympathetic to the problems of his mother, and actively resentful toward Howard, his stepfather.

"Perhaps the mistake I made with my stepfather was to have missed a father too dearly. I wanted to fill a void, to fit an image that was unrealistic. I felt painfully left out with my friends who were always bragging, 'My father once played minor league ball; my father has medals from the war; my father . . . this and that.' I wanted a hero also. When Howard failed to meet my expectations, I took it out on him and everyone surrounding me. This was the beginning of a conflict that would last for many years. I built a protective shelter around me, my family, and friends. I would not accept my stepfather as simply an average Joe who was married to my mother."

Just as Jeffrey's strong needs interfered with a harmonious relationship, Howard's unmet needs for an "ideal" son also presented obstacles. Jeffrey wasn't a particularly strong child, nor was he quick-witted or athletic. Yet his stepfather frequently made it clear that these were important qualities in a boy. On one occasion, Jeffrey was matched with his cousin—Howard's nephew—in boxing. He felt forced into it; Howard insisted—"He needs to learn to handle himself"—despite the protestations of his wife. The other boy was everything Jeffrey wasn't—quick to catch on, strong, and very graceful. The whole event left Jeffrey feeling awkward and ashamed.

On another occasion, at dinner, Howard asked Jeffrey how school was going. After talking awhile about his classes and friends, Jeffrey reported, casually but with barely concealed pleasure, how he had dropped into the school lounge one afternoon and asked someone there if he wanted to play chess.

"It was a good game but I beat him without too much difficulty. . . . Then I found out he was the captain of the school's chess team."

There was a long pause, and then Howard intoned, "Some captain!" Jeffrey deeply resented his stepfather's denigration of his achievements and magnification of his deficiencies. Conflicts between the two occurred frequently.

"We lived in a stable but poor area of Brooklyn during my growing-up years. This was the atmosphere I was used to; it was also the backdrop of my emotional traumas. Perhaps a change would prove beneficial—actually it did—but when Howard announced we were moving to Long Island, I hated him even more. I was scared, outraged, and confused when we moved. Life seemed even more gloomy and depressing. I was in a new town, a new lifestyle. It was frightening. I wondered how I would make new friends. I didn't think people would accept me. Slowly, though, things started to improve. During the first year, things didn't change too much. Howard and I were still on the outs, my schoolwork was poor, and I felt stifled. This time, however, I was not giving up. Something made me want to succeed; I don't know whether it was the new atmosphere, maturity, or what. In any case, life began to improve."

It wasn't until midadolescence that Jeffrey's relationship with his stepfather began to show signs of moving in a more positive direction. As a young man of nineteen, socially successful and with his childhood perspective broadened, he sees things differently.

"Finally I can look at the troubled aspects of my childhood with some objectivity. Most of those distressing feelings are gone, even though some vestiges still remain; there are various feelings that I still hold, but to a much lesser extent. I will always wonder what it would have been like if my father had lived. I still feel cheated in losing him. But I no longer expect Howard to pick up where my father left off. Deep inside, I think I always knew that this was, and always will be, impossible. Now I accept it. I also recognize and appreciate my mother for having been tremendously supportive in her own quiet, persistent way. As for Howard, he, over the years, has also changed. I no longer have to perform to be acceptable to him. Ironically, our clashes were for similar reasons—we both insisted on changing the other to a cherished fantasy rather than relating to the actual person."

Some children are adamant in their distaste for a stepparent; time does not heal wounds or add to understanding. Occasionally the child genuinely dislikes the stepparent as a person. More often the child is still close to the removed parent and is worried about being disloyal, feels the stepparent does not compare favorably to some fantasized ideal, or fears the remaining parent's close relationship with another will be a source of deprivation—"Does my Mother (Father) still love me? If she (he) does, why did she (he) marry again?" There is also the child who is initially aloof but somewhat willing to interact with the stepparent; this child can be won over. A stepparent who likes him or her makes it possible. Another reaction is one in which the child, usually younger, is ready and willing to accept the stepparent as parent.

For the majority, troubling and recurrent questions arise: "What is this new person to me? What am I to him (her)? Can I like this new stepparent and still love my other parent?" A whirl of uncertainties surround the child.

"The stepparent," Anne Simon writes in *Stepchild in the Family,* "is in a position unlike any other the child knows; not parent, not teacher, not housekeeper or grandmother, not uncle, doctor or family friend, but with something of all these functions, he is uniquely related to the child by its parent's marriage." Given the confusion as to how each is to relate to the other, the choosing of titles ("What should I call him?") can highlight the ambivalence. Mrs. Simon comments:

The most sophisticated parent stumbles over the introduction, "This is my son and this is my stepson." Adjust the inequality with "These are my sons," and the villainy is compounded; real and stepson feel put upon with equal parts hostility and vengeance. Children mumble a suggestive "This is my father and this is his. . ." allowing silence and a wave of the hand to finish the sentence.

The child sees things dramatically differently from the adult. For the adult, remarriage may, at least to some extent, expunge the former mate; for the child, there is no such thing as an ex-father or ex-mother. He has a protected image of a parent, alive or dead, in his mind, and this new person is not about to be an instant replacement. One stepchild, filled with apprehension when confronted with a new family member, put it this way:

"I was six years old when my father died. After one year, my mother married again. I remember very vividly how one day a strange new man was introduced to me; I was told he would be living with us and that I should call him 'Daddy.' I thought to myself, 'How can I call him Father? I don't feel like he is my father.' The word stuck in my throat. How can 'This is your new father magically translate into a relationship? This man, my stepfather, stood there, probably feeling as awkward as I, and waited for my utterance. And I waited also. Would he reach out to me; would he do something that would make the word 'father' flow more easily? He didn't. He stood and waited, as I did. At seventeen, after several years of being wary of each other, the stalemate has finally dissolved. We are not father and son but we are close."

Remarriage creates not only new parental relationships but also new sibling relationships. Sometimes two sets of children, one from the man's former family and one from the woman's, are brought together in the same household. This means that some families are going to be a mixture of brothers and sisters, stepbrothers and stepsisters, and possibly later half-brothers and half-sisters, all living under one roof. Remarriage doesn't always include children from so many quarters; frequently the father's children are weekend visitors and the mother's children are permanent residents. In either event, these children are suddenly thrust into relationships with one another and are expected to get along.

In every family, there are periods when brothers and sisters are competitive with each other; it often happens that they eventually grow closer. In remarriage, because not all the children grow up with each other and because there has been a drastic reordering of their lives, their relationship is very likely to begin in jealousy, competion for favor, and measuring each against the other. Getting used to new ways and new stepsiblings is bound to create conflict.

Robert was eleven years old when his mother remarried. He is now twenty-one and in his last semester of college.

"At first, I was really looking forward to having a new brother, but Jeff and I turned out to be very different—real opposites. I felt uncomfortable with him. He was very proper and I was very casual. We were like the odd couple. We fought all the time. I was more of a scrapper both physically and verbally, so I usually got my way. I let out my feelings easily—you could always tell what was going on with me. He kept things inside and didn't talk. My real brother, Eddie, who was fourteen, and my stepbrother were on even worse terms. Most times they didn't talk at all. I think Eddie saw Jeff as a real sissy and couldn't be bothered with him.

". . . I also didn't like sharing my room with Jeff. I could just picture him thinking, 'Robert is a real slob,' and I didn't want to be under his silent scrutiny. Most of all I wasn't happy having to share my mother. Sometimes I wished it were just the three of us: my mother, Eddie, and me. As for playing favorites, I think my mother and my stepfather tried to be fair. Although when things had to be done, my stepfather seemed to ask Eddie or me much more than he asked Jeff. My mother developed a system to equalize things in some ways. She would take each one of us to a movie or something each week. We took turns getting unshared attention. I liked that. We all did. At one point, we started to have family meetings to talk things out. That helped. But I'm still, to this day, closer to Eddie. And I still can't take

Jeff for too long. I do think, though, that we were successful in forming one family. My relationship with him is one of peaceful coexistence. It is not unlike many of my friends' relationships with their natural siblings."

In many instances, stepbrothers and stepsisters get along very well; as with biological brothers and sisters, there is a potential for good and bad relations. Relationships may be loving at one point, cordial at another, and violent at yet another. Again, there is a parallel to biological siblings. While stepsiblings have conflicts, they also have reason to move close: They have a common heritage and therefore are desirous of the reassurance that comes from finding that another shares their feelings of loneliness, confusion, and resentment. The scarce research on the subject of stepsiblings points to one clear trend: If parents have a successful marital relationship and if the stepparents have good relations with their stepchild, then stepsiblings are more likely to have good relationships with each other.

## Implications

The stepchild drama unfolds in three acts. Act One: The marriage into which the child was born is dissolved through death or divorce. Act Two: The child and the remaining parent reorganize their lives as a result of the loss. Act Three: The parent remarries, requiring the child to make a third major emotional adjustment. The implications of this sequence of events are complex and far from completely known. An easily applied set of rules for guidance does not exist; there are too many exceptions and too much relativity. Some general observations, however, do apply.

1. *Loss:* The problems children have in comprehending the death of a parent are magnified when the remaining parent is reluctant to discuss the matter with them. The adjustment will take a healthier course if, as far as the children's intellectual

development permits, they are given honest answers about what dying means. Many parents admit they do not adequately explain a death to their children because they are afraid they cannot do so without becoming very upset. Enmeshed in their own grief, they decide to shield the child. This is a mistake. Not talking to a child about the death of a loved one does not offer protection. Every child is shocked by the death of a parent even if the reaction is not apparent. To inhibit or evade a child's questions about death is to enhance his sense of confusion. When this occurs, children make up their own fantasies and "facts"—"Something could also happen to me; Mommy (Daddy) will also leave me"—to explain the "mystery."

Here is a capsuled dialogue that might take place:

Young child: What happened to Daddy?
Mother: He is very sick and will be gone a long, long time.

Young child: *(crying)* I miss Daddy.
Mother: He has gone away.

Young child: *(continuing to cry)* I want Daddy.
Mother: *(trying to control herself)* Stop crying right now. You're becoming too upset.

In this exchange, there is the pretension that the dead parent is only gone and therefore may return at some future time. This will only compound the child's confusion, inhibit grief, and thereby delay the mourning process. In addition, there is an attempt to cut off the child's reaction, possibly because the mother is afraid of becoming upset herself. This is disadvantageous to mother and child. The emotions accompanying the loss of a loved one—sadness, regret, anger—demand to be acknowledged. Discouraging free expression seriously impairs the process of adaptation. This mother, by crying and showing her sadness in front of the child, would be setting a healthy example: "It is all right to admit you are sad because of Daddy's death."

A replay of the dialogue with a more effective approach might take this form:

Young child: What happened to Daddy?
Mother: He is dead. He will not be with us anymore.

Young child: *(crying)* I miss Daddy.
Mother: *(crying)* I know, sweetheart, I do too. But I will take very good care of you. I love you.

Young child: *(continuing to cry)* Will I ever see Daddy again?
Mother: No, darling. Daddy is dead and you will not see him again.

The guideline of honesty and attention to feelings also applies to a loss of a parent through divorce. The adults in these families should make certain that the divorce has been simply and honestly interpreted to the child. Secrecy and evasion will often do what they are intended to prevent. If the child cannot know the truth as the parent sees it, he will misunderstand the divorce, feel his parents were mean to him, worry that he caused the split, and feel threatened by a recurrence of these feelings in the event of a remarriage.

There are limits to disclosure, of course. The child's image of the other parent should not be damaged. More effective communication will inform the child that "Daddy and Mommy were fighting so much they decided it was better not to live in the same house anymore." It should also be emphasized that the youngster is in no way responsible for the divorce—"Daddy (Mommy) did not go away because of anything you did; divorces happen when grown-ups decide they are not happy with each other anymore; and after trying a lot, they are not able to get happy together." A little child also needs the frequent reassurance that the remaining parent will protect him and that the removed parent still loves him, even though he is not going to be living in the same house any longer.

2. *Between Marriages:* An adult who loses a marital

partner has opportunities to interact with numerous other adults and, in the process, to find a replacement. The child has fewer options—he is not in a position to "look around." Children have only the remaining parent to rely on and to invest their emotions in. Both parent and child are needy. The remaining parent is likely to wish he were someplace else—it is much easier to deal with personal problems without the presence of children.

During the interval between marriages, the parents who are most nurturant are usually seen by their children as supportive of them when the going gets tough, able to empathize with their feelings, and willing to accept them as unique individuals. This precludes the demand that "You must think, feel, and act like me." In contrast, the parents who are most damaging are usually characterized by such negative qualities as low are usually characterized by such negative qualities as low self-esteem, indecisiveness, and the inclination to be self-deprecating. It is not an absolute that if a parent feels negative, the children will necessarily be disturbed, however; some children who live in an unusually stormy and conflicted family develop particularly adaptive, effective, and sturdy personalities. One small-scale study, for example, compared children in intact and broken families and found those in the latter category to have developed to a greater degree traits and habits potentially useful in coping with life problems. But if one thinks in terms of probabilities, there is an increased chance of a disturbed parent ending up with a disturbed child.

A parent who finds that he is chronically irritated, distant from his child, or forever giving the child negative feedback can be fairly certain things aren't going well. The quality of time spent with the child—ranging from pleasant and relaxed to abrasive and tense—is another detectable indicator. Feeling "I wish they would get lost" not sometimes, but often, is also an obvious signal. The presence—or absence—of warmth and closeness is apparent to any moderately sensitive person. Using indices such as these, most parents can estimate how satisfactory their relationship with their children is. Between marriages, parents would be wise to monitor their interaction with their children and take seriously their own intuition about what is going on between the children and themselves—parents are frequently good judges. If there is an extended period of interaction (several months) that feels destructive, parents should be prepared to secure extra support or guidance for the children and themselves. Relatives, particularly grandparents, can provide needed nurturance for the children. Professional assistance may also be advisable for both parent and child.

Despite the hardships, emotional pitfalls, and practical burdens of becoming uncoupled, many single parents seem to rear their children reasonably well—possibly not so well as happily married couples, but probably better than unhappily married ones. Fathers, who are usually the absent parent, may be warmer and more relaxed with their children than they were during the stressful period of breaking up; mothers, as well, may be greatly relieved at having dissolved a painful relationship.

All in all, it is not much more difficult to be a single parent than it is to be a good friend or marital partner. An important ingredient is emotional health. Those parents who have been slowly but consistently growing emotionally usually improve as parents with the passage of time, for as they become increasingly whole and balanced people, it is natural for them to be increasingly effective in many roles—including that of the single parent.

3. *Remarriage:* As much as parents would like it to occur sooner, a child's adjustment to a new marriage often takes two or three years, sometimes longer. Children must be allowed this time rather than be forced to feel things they don't yet (and may never) feel. In addition to the manner in which the loss and interval between marriages was handled, the psychological condition of the child to begin with can either magnify or minimize the reaction to remarriage. A child who can cope with life's difficulties adequately will almost certainly react better to divorce and remarriage than the chronically insecure child. For the more psychologically fragile child, professional counseling may be warranted. Early detection and intervention in these in-

stances increases the chances that the child will attain a reasonable sense of well-being. Whether the child is fragile or secure, or somewhere in between, a number of suggestions merit consideration:

a) A man or woman who has lost a spouse and subsequently meets someone who seems to be a prospect for remarriage should carefully assess how that person will fit in with the children in the family. This is a very critical issue and one that can be sensibly evaluated by observing how the children and the prospect get along with each other in a variety of situations. If, after weeks of contact between them, tension and unpleasant feelings are prominent, this is a bad sign and bodes ill for the children.

b) Children require preparation for remarriage. Springing a marriage announcement on them as a last-minute surprise does not give them time to absorb the plans into their own lives. They should be invited to discuss their feelings, fantasies, and expectations regarding the new relationship. Parents would do well to listen sensitively to their children's thoughts about remarriage.

c) Children desire frequent and continued reassurance of their place in the family. While reassurance can be demonstrated verbally, it can also sometimes be more dramatically and effectively shown through action. For example, a child may desire to spend the major portion of the day with his parent. This can be an important request and a test of the parent's availability. It is important to respect the feelings inherent in such requests and to honor them when feasible.

d) Finally, it is heartening to note that children are flexible. Healthy children have the capacity to bend with life. Their minds are not stiff, they are able to sway and not crack. Remarriage, despite its complexity, is weathered by most. Although the periods when children are sorting things out in their minds can be rugged on themselves as well as on the adults in their lives, the number of children who do not make a successful adjustment to a new marriage is quite small.

# 6
# The Impact of "Instant" Children on Marriage

## Rude Awakening

"The beginning of our relationship was absolutely beautiful and very romantic. Joan was a blind date arranged through a lawyer who was our mutual friend. I don't ordinarily make blind dates but my friend really urged me on this one. He was right! We went to dinner but never noticed the food. We couldn't talk enough, we got misty-eyed again and again, we were so enraptured with each other. Joan and I went back to my apartment and talked and necked almost all night. After having been single for four years, I had had plenty of relationships that were mostly sexual but I knew this one was different, and so did Joan. After three months, when I asked her to marry me, she wasn't surprised—it was just natural and inevitable.

"Although I had met Joan's two boys—they seemed kind of wild—and spent time with them before we were married, I didn't give them an awful lot of thought. Neither, it seems, did Joan. Her mother looked after them quite often and we were so consumed in ourselves that they became mere background. We were able to spend several weekends away together and really had a ball. We were carefree and jubilant. The search for a soulmate was over. There did not appear to be any major issues confronting us. Money wasn't a problem—my former wife was remarried, and since we had no children, my obligation to her was nil—and we felt very much in love. Isn't that enough? I thought so.

"Then reality set in. Boy, were we mistaken. Shortly after we were married, Joan's mother moved to Florida and for the first time both of us realized 'Hey, there are two kids here that are very, very demanding.' Steven's problem—anger about the change in his life brought on by the marriage—unsteadied and shook everything in the neat little world we had created. Not only were we both preoccupied with him, we began to snipe at each other over stupid things. The tension was immense. The emotional vibes were terrible. After a year or so, I was practically suicidal over the situation. So was Joan. The marriage was being drained; it was really under fire. It had to be—we spent all our time discussing him, our other son Alan, and reeling under the onslaught of problems. I couldn't even walk into a room occupied by one of the boys without being the recipient of hateful looks. And it wasn't just the stepfather thing; Joan got her share of misery dumped on her also. With our dreams of 'one happy family' quickly dissolving, both of us began to wonder—first silently, then out loud—if we had used poor judgment in getting married.

"The situation was getting worse by the day. I was withdrawing, Joan was sullen, and the boys varied in degrees of hostility. One Saturday morning, while preparing breakfast, I took a realistic look at the boys. Joan had already left for her class. Both boys were grumbling about inconsequential matters. I was suddenly struck by the control they had over our lives. Usually mild-mannered, I let go with a blast: 'You two have been acting like spoiled brats. The time of coddling is over. Steven, you are going to start behaving [I spelled out the specifics for him] or else lose the privileges you now enjoy. Alan, the same goes for you!' With that, I marched out of the kitchen feeling better than I had in weeks. The boys were left at the table, stunned by my proclamations. I know this approach goes against all the child-care books and articles that advise people to use tender loving care. At this point, though, those instructions would have been phony because my explosion rocked those kids back to reality. We sat down later in the day with Joan present and had a 'family meeting.' We talked about their feelings—the anger, jealousy, and bitterness. Joan and I listened, aired our views, and developed some simple household rules that were to be abided by. This was the beginning of an improved all-around relationship. And it came just in time. If we had continued in the direction we were going, our marriage would have been beyond repair."

The pressure from children on a remarriage is tremendous. Some of us, like Joan and her husband, enter a new marriage—the first, second, or third—with blind optimism. "Everything is going to be beautiful between us. We are in love, so why concern ourselves with the boring details of everyday living." Captured by the myth of romantic love, we expect too much too soon, and know too little about what is required to meet the awaiting challenge. It is not hard to understand why this happens. Having looked forward to a new day—a time of commitment and companionship after a period of single parenthood—the power of love seems awesome indeed.

Love is an important emotion; certainly it is one of the most powerful forces in human nature. But love is also frail and can easily deteriorate under a barrage of "everyday" obstacles. The two prime obstacles to love feelings in a first marriage are money and children—in that order. The problems in a subsequent marriage are similar, but the order is reversed. Children are a bigger issue because they are *there,* unlike in a first marriage when a couple can have several years to themselves to develop a relationship before they decide to have children.

Childless couples who remarry share the same advantage. That is, they have the opportunity to adjust to each other, work out a living pattern, and enjoy each other's exclusive attention. If they eventually create a child, they will very likely have already established a critical bond between themselves. This luxury is not available to couples when the children exist from the outset. These couples experience lack of privacy, mental as well as physical. Children's needs demand to be met and tension often runs high in the new household.

Satisfaction with remarriage may well depend on how well husband and wife can parent without allowing the children to become divisive influences in their lives. This is not always easy. For instance, stepparents and parents may have opposing views on how to bring up children and will disagree over which policy to pursue. Children are experts at playing off one adult against the other in these circumstances. In other instances, even the most agreeable, blameless child can inadvertently stir up distressing jealousy by resembling an absent parent or being viewed by a stepparent as a competitor.

Some parents become trapped in a conflict of loyalty between their children and their mate; the strain can be enormous, and if not eased, the deterioration of their marital relationship is inevitable. Others do not reveal their feelings about the marital relationship directly but shift the brunt of their grievance to issues involving the children. The children, too, may misdirect efforts by purposely distracting husband and wife when conflict erupts. In this chapter, divisive issues—the apparent and the more subtle—involving the children will be considered.

## Divisive Dilemmas

### Discipline

Should authority over the children be divided equally between parent and stepparent? What type of discipline should be administered? What role will punishment play? Child-discipline procedures seem to be the most formidable problem between biological and stepparents. Some stepparents, especially those who have never parented before, feel timid about disciplining their stepchildren and relinquish authority to the biological parent. A typical comment: "I work at keeping a lid on my feelings.

When I'm annoyed or don't want to be bothered, I feel uneasy saying, 'Beat it,' to my stepchildren; they didn't ask me to be here." Some biological parents resent any interference by the stepparent. In a dispute about a child, they may pull rank by saying, "You don't really understand him, you weren't around during the important years of his development."

Where a stepparent is concerned, a youngster can have an ulterior motive for misbehaving. Particularly in the beginning stage of the relationship with his new stepparent, a resentful or frightened youngster may figure that if he provokes his new stepparent to anger, he can provide evidence that will convince his mother to send him away. In other instances, he may seek to test the stepparent's liking for him. In either case, he baits the stepparent, and the stepparent, being neither saint nor sage, is likely to bite. The pattern is classic.

Robert, nine years old, was playing with his stepfather's stamp collection. On earlier occasions, he had been warned not to play with the stamps—some of which are extremely fragile and valuable—and, as a compromise, he was given a collection of his own. But Robert, because he was annoyed with his stepfather, Jack, did not heed the warning and one of the older, more brittle stamps was destroyed by his handling.

Jack was furious: "I am cutting your allownace for six months. You are not watching TV for two weeks, and you are going to stay in your room after school and all evening for the rest of the month, you little brat!"

Robert went straight to his mother to set the stage for his defense. It worked. Robert's mother opened with, "How dare you treat him like that!" An argument raged, which effectively discouraged Jack from interacting with his stepson. Mother was in the middle. Any comments by either party went through her. As a result, the relationship between Jack and his wife became discordant. His wife felt he had unfairly withdrawn. Jack didn't see it that way. He felt demeaned and powerless; he was resentful that she did not trust and support him. In the meantime, Robert's disruptive behavior worsened.

Questions about who is to be in charge and what disciplinary action is to be taken are difficult to answer. However, unless the dilemma is openly acknowledged and a mutually agreeable way to discipline is developed, a couple is likely to engage in some ugly battles throughout their marriage. Even an exchange of ideas about discipline that results in no more than a clarification of differences can be helpful. It is part of getting to know a mate. An individual's views on discipline do not exist in isolation; they are an expression of values—what is desirable, what is undesirable, what degree of self-control is allowed, what behavior influences others, and so forth.

Stepparents under discipline restrictions would be wise to discuss their feelings of frustration, anger, and injustice because, if denied, these feelings will eventually undermine the marriage. It is also unhealthy for the children to be disciplined only by the biological parent because this encourages parental divisiveness.

Stepparent and mate should discuss their serious disciplinary disagreements privately. Children in stepfamilies are particularly sensitive to these issues and are likely to use some statements as ammunition against one of the parents. However, after the initial groundwork is laid, the entire family should participate in the development of clear and reasonable household rules. If the agree disciplinary procedures are jointly enforced in such a way as to prevent the children from pitting one spouse against the other, then disciplinary problems will prove to be manageable and even educational.

## Jealousy

When a marriage results in combining families, jealousy can make problems that are ordinarily hard to resolve seem impossible. During the early period of the remarriage, there are likely to be many kinds of demands from the youngsters, demands that are in reality bids for reassurance. It takes time for children to trust that they will get the help and support they need as best as it can be provided. Sometimes the adults make an overall statement to this effect at the outset: "We're going to do our best to treat everybody fairly, to work out things satisfactorily for all of us, even though the going may be rough at first."

Such a statement will have most impact when the youngsters actually experience it as reality. Once they feel they are in a secure, nurturant environment, their demands will drop off and so will the jealousy toward each other that usually accompanies insecurity. There are families, though, that struggle with a different kind of jealousy, not between children but between a stepparent and a child.

Mrs. Steele, a widow with a daughter aged ten, married a widower with a thirteen-year-old girl. After a few weeks, the girls adjusted to each other and got along well. Beth, the older girl, was the more attractive of the two, but this did not seem to bother Marge, who was content to admire Beth as a glamorous older sister. Neither was Marge upset by Beth's popularity or her excellent school achievement. On the contrary, she viewed Beth as an ideal to which she aspired.

While Marge was not bothered by her stepsister's outstanding characteristics, Mrs. Steele was. She could not admit her jealousy, but it was apparent in her hypercritical attitude toward Beth almost from the beginning of the marriage. Mrs. Steele was hard on Beth. Whether it was a matter of table manners, the tidiness of her room or her dress, she usually had something sarcastic or nasty to say about her. Beth's efforts to fight back only further provoked Mrs. Steele. Even her own daughter's interventions went unheeded. Mr. Steele, quite disturbed by the harsh treatment of his daughter, was becoming increasingly fed up, and by the year's end, the marriage was in serious trouble.

Mrs. Steele's problem is not uncommon. Jealousy becomes an issue when the child is an unwanted reminder of a spouse's first love, when a youngster makes one feel inadequate as a parent, or when the stepchild is regarded as a competitor for the spouse's love. There are several remedies a couple can apply to alleviate stepparent–child jealousy.

To begin with, it is important for the jealous stepparent to become aware that it is not the child's behavior but his own attitude that is the problem. An understanding rather than confrontive, blame-oriented spouse is more likely to promote this realization. A stepparent is likely to be very sensitive about this issue and having his feelings understood can mean a great deal. It will also provide an atmosphere in which the stepparent can explore the basis of his or her negative attitude. In contrast, blame and harshness will add to defensiveness and most certainly worsen the situation.

Once a stepparent can acknowledge the problem nondefensively, he or she is in a position to view the situation from the child's perspective. This can be very useful. Mrs. Steele, for example, could consider what it must mean to Beth to have wanted a mother so long and then to have one who is so critical of her. She might also think about the difficulty Beth experiences in sharing her father. If a stepparent can enter the youngster's world and see the stepchild as a *child* who needs help rather than as threatening evidence of a former spouse or as a competitor, the problems are likely to be understood and solved.

The chances are that empathic discussion, admission of the source of the negativism, and an effort to act more positively can at least minimize jealousy to the point where the child is not damaged and the marriage is not put in jeopardy.

## Conflict of Loyalty

Karen, a thirty-five-year-old divorcée, has been remarried two years. Her husband, Martin, is a successful attorney and a bright, serious man. Despite their obvious affection toward each other, Karen is having a hard time of it. She considers the marriage to be workable, but in an emotion-filled conversation, she discussed her distress:

"I feel as if I'm being pulled apart. I am constantly having to decide, plan, make choices, cut corners to find time for everybody. If I spend time alone with the children, I feel as if Martin is being left out. If I spend time with Martin, the children act as if I'm being disloyal or something. Although my first marriage was stormy, the children were his too, and there wasn't the conflict. It's ridiculous. I thought marrying Martin would bring a steadiness and calmness to our home and, as a result, make mothering easier. Instead, I feel under more stress now than in my single days. It's sad to say, but when Martin goes on a business trip, things are much more relaxed. There is more spontaneity, everyone's more at ease. Somehow when I don't shove the kids into the background to attend to Martin, they are less demanding—even if I am off in another room reading.

"I want the marriage to work, but I constantly find myself in the middle, orchestrating everybody's happiness. When Martin's two children come on weekends and mix with my two, things really become precarious. Sometimes I just sit around wondering, 'How do other remarried parents manage? Is this really what family life is all about?' There's such competition for attention, I feel like a juggler. I'm so tired of trying to keep the whole act in harmony. I don't know what to do. I would never forgive the children if the marriage didn't work. If I gave up custody of the children, I couldn't live with myself and I would always hold Martin responsible. I have this recurring dream that we are all running from something terribly frightening and all the other family members want me to keep up with them, but as hard as I try, I can't move. The result is they all run off in different directions and I'm left alone. The dream really reflects how I feel—stuck!"

Karen's feelings are shared by many remarried parents. The pressure to fulfill the needs of the children and of each other, particularly during the first few years of marriage, frequently results in increased distance rather than closeness among family members. It isn't long before the marital partners are frustrated and disappointed at the deterioration of their love for each other. Work, household responsibilities, and the demands of the children take up most of their time, leaving them little energy for each other.

Frequently, as was the case with Karen, a parent, during years of being single, becomes accustomed to meeting the children's needs exclusively. After remarriage, the youngsters continue to turn to that parent only for advice and assistance, and conflicts of loyalty develop. Many stepparents report that when they are alone with the children, things go much better. For one thing, the element of competition is removed. For another, the stepparent has a greater opportunity to ease into the closed system. This suggests that in situations of this kind, leaving the children alone with the stepparent is a useful tactic. Aside from the benefits to the stepparent–child relationship, it gives the biological parent an opportunity to trust the nurturance of the children to the spouse.

Conflicts of loyalty are usually accompanied by misconceptions of what children need. They may *want* constant attention but they don't need it. Actually, spending too much physical and emotional energy on children undermines their self-reliance as well as the marital relationship. It is important that children learn that parents require some privacy. And it is important that parents make provisions for time alone.

## Destructive Distractors: Children as Weapons/Buffers

Sometimes the impact of children on marriage can be deceptive. The real war is between the parents; youngsters merely provide the battleground. This can occur in a primary marriage, but is more likely to happen in a subsequent one where the pressure to succeed is overwhelming and negative emotions are denied. Frequently such feelings are transferred to other people or events. This process of "blamemanship" or "scapegoating" usually leaves both partners infuriated and baffled.

A parental fight about disciplinary practices, for example, may mask a more intimate issue the couple does not dare confront. Rob and Florence Vogel have been married three years. They live with Florence's two children by her previous marriage. The Vogels, in recent months, have had a dialogue similar to the following with increasing frequency.

SHE: You have to start being more of a disciplinarian with the kids. They are not shaping up and you don't intervene strongly enough.

HE: *(irritated)* Here we go again. You know how important it is for me to relate well to the kids. Why do I have to be the heavy?

SHE: *(insistent)* Relating well is one thing, but I want you to be the authority in this house and you are being too lax.

HE: *(angry)* I'm not too lax, that's stupid! I discipline the kids and deal with them just fine.

SHE: Oh, bull! Who disciplines the kids? Me! Who takes all the responsibility for discipline? Me!

HE: Yeah, you act just like a cop with them. And what does it get you? They really...

SHE: *(angrily interrupting)* That's my point. You let me do all the dirty work. That makes me the "mean mother" and you the "good guy." It angers me to no end. You just won't cooperate!

HE: *(pacing and frustrated)* Florence, you make it sound as if I don't guide the kids, as if I'm a nonentity. Damnit, that's just not true. Why shouldn't you like it when the kids and I relate well? They're good kids and I am very pleased with how they are growing up. What the hell do you want?

SHE: *(disgusted)* But I can't do it all. You have to back me up and you never do! Listen to what happened just before you came home yesterday...

HE: Forget it! I don't want to hear it.

SHE: *(righteously)* Why? You see, that's what I mean! You don't want to take part...

HE: *(counterattacking)* You bitch! I hate it when you use me this way. In fact, I can't stand it. I refuse to continue talking about it.

It developed, after further discussion, that Florence was jealous of her own children because Rob's relationship with them was so close. She felt he was more attentive and tender to them than he was to her. As she put it in a later conversation, "How could I admit that I was jealous? In my first marriage, I felt my husband's first love was his business and I took a very distant second place. The thought that I was involved in a variation of the same drama was horrifying. I can see why my emotions were expressed in a disguised manner, I felt so vulnerable."

Rob, in turn, did indeed withdraw from Florence. Not because he didn't love her, however. What turned him off was her constant tattling on the children, characterizing them as brats, and insisting that he be a strict disciplinarian. This aroused a strong memory of ugly, angry emotions from his past. Rob's ex-wife used to constantly badger him about his son's misdeeds and demand that he beat discipline into him. To Rob, this was like a recurring nightmare from the past with a very frightening theme: "She does not really love me, I am only being used as a father for her kids." As the Vogels began to level about their real feelings, wants, expectations, and fears, the spiral of misconceptions they held collapsed and the issue of disciplining the children dissolved.

A related ploy using disciplinary practice as a subterfuge occurs when a parent states, "I want you to be an equal partner in the care of the children," but simultaneously gives secret signals to the children that undermine the mate's authority. People in stepfamilies are particularly susceptible to these types of double messages.

In one instance, a stepfather and his wife agreed that their teenage son stayed out too late on school nights. Yet when his stepson arrived home very late one night and he reacted firmly, the boy's mother offered to set out her son's clothes and make him breakfast so that he could sleep a little later in the morning.

On other occasions, just as puzzling to the stepfather, his wife acted in complete contradiction to their initial agreement on what was the "right" action to take and how to take it.

After what seemed like endless arguing, the stepfather threatened to pull out, to completely withdraw from family participation. At this point, his wife, also under a severe strain, broke down and honestly confronted her behavior. She acknowledged negative feelings toward her husband. These feelings, having built up over several months, had become very frightening; in her view, they threatened the relationship. As a protective measure, she had sabotaged her husband's efforts to enter the "closed system" she had formed with her son. Unfortunately, the solution she chose served only to confuse her son, to provoke negativism in her husband, and to increase her frustration.

Another displacement strategy using the children as an overt issue to cover up hostility or hurt is "rejection collecting." Sexual inadequacy was his first wife's complaint against Carl Mason. One night the current Mrs. Mason did not feel particularly sexy and refused her husband's advances. Rather than talk about his feelings in this sensitive area, Mr. Mason stewed. The next day when Mrs. Mason returned home from an afternoon of grocery shopping, she found the house in total disarray. Her husband, who had been left in charge of their three children, secretly delighted in her obvious furor. Stunned at first by the utter chaos, Mrs. Mason carried in her heavy shopping bags and began to clean the kitchen table, pick up the toys strewn about, and wipe the spilled drinks from the floor. Upstairs, the TV was blaring and the children were fully absorbed. Feeling like an exploited slave, she muttered to herself, "God, this is a drag! What the hell is going on? This is ridiculous!" With that, she charged upstairs, turned off the TV, and furiously confronted her children: "You are an inconsiderate bunch! Get downstairs and clean up your mess!"

At this moment, Mr. Mason, who had been waiting patiently for his sweet revenge, appeared and was requested by his wife to intercede. In complying with his wife's request, Mr. Mason allowed his children to see that he was condescending to their mother. He implied, "My heart isn't really in this but I'd better say these things to get your mother off our backs."

By admonishing his children in this transparently superficial manner, Mr. Mason baited the trap further, thereby escalating his revenge. The unknowing partner walking into the trap is provoked into an unreasonable rage and is misled as to its basis. The immediate purpose (hurting the partner, "evening the score," avoiding closeness) has been achieved. In the longer run, of course, Mr. Mason and other "injustice" or "rejection collectors" widen the gap between themselves and their family to the detriment of all.

"Buffering," yet another distractor, is initiated by the children and reinforced by the marital partners. It is not unusual for a child to drift into the role of mediator in the new marriage. In the previous marriage, the child may have been so enmeshed in the discord of his parents that he assumed responsibility for peacemaking. In the new union, he becomes a buffer because he cannot tolerate the conflict ("If they split, where does that leave me?"), and because his parents, sharing a similar fear of their own, become dependent on the child mediator to maintain an illusion of tranquility between them. The following conversation involving a child and his parents illustrates the process.

HUSBAND: Damnit, Gail, I get so angry when you spend enormous sums of money on such ridiculous crap.
WIFE: That's just like you. When I spend money, it's ridiculous. When you buy something, it's a necessity. You see things in such a one-sided way.
CHILD: I got into a fight in school today and I had to sit in the principal's office.
WIFE: Michael, you shouldn't be fighting. Someone could get hurt.
HUSBAND: If there's a problem in school, you tell the teacher. Don't use your hands on anybody. The teacher will help you talk it out. Okay?

Masquerading as a "naughty child" this youngster produces well-timed interventions to set himself up as a target and to divert his mother and father from further argument. He has learned that if he can turn their attention toward him, they will automatically issue a truce with each other. Parents who are fearful of losing their relationship, who prefer appearance to real intimacy, are likely to be willing collaborators and reinforcers of the child's efforts. However, temporary armistices achieved this way are likely to have a damaging effect on the youngster. Once he is accepted in the role of peacemaker, he may feel at fault every time there is an emotional eruption he has failed to prevent. Continued distress between parents will result in escalated anxiety and disappointment in the child.

Instead of being supported and nurtured by his parents, the "child peacemaker" has very prematurely assumed an adult role. In effect, the child gives up his childhood to keep the peace. The effort is futile.

This practice, and the others described and their numerous variations, allow marriage partners to show superiority, cover up guilt feelings, hurt a mate, avoid intimacy, achieve superficial closeness, feel justified in "giving up," and so on. All these ends are shortsighted and the tactics are self- and relationship-defeating because they conceal rather than clarify the real issues. Strong feelings of jealousy, guilt, insecurity, and resentment, if not discussed openly, drain a relationship. If one partner feels the other would become alarmed or defensive about these burning issues, then talking to another remarried parent or nonjudgmental friend is suggested. If these outlets are unavailable, professional help should be sought.

## The Coping Process

Everyone who remarries has the usual difficulties of starting over—setting up a new home, budgeting finances, and adjusting to another person's lifestyle and habits. In one sense, adjustment in a second or subsequent marriage may be smoother because at least one party has gone through the process before; but if children are present, as we have seen, there are bound to

## The Impact of "Instant" Children

be difficulties. Even if the transition to a new marriage is unimpeded, the new lovers have a big job ahead of them. Children, particularly when they have spent a period alone with one parent, dislike change and are likely to be disrupted by the union. Husband and wife are also affected by the reorganization. As a consequence, many of the normal emotional events of family life become exaggerated.

For example, in any family, spouses have a relationship in which the children are not included. It is common for children to try to get between parents to reap some of that special attention. In the reconstituted family, with husband and wife very intent on developing their young relationship, children are more frustrated in this task and parents, guiltier than usual, can succumb to their manipulations. This is a disservice to all involved. The struggle may be somewhat unpleasant, but the frustration the child experiences (along with love and understanding) is a vital force in his growth. Ideally, by not succeeding in coming between his parents, he is pushed toward emotional independence and toward forming other relationships in his life. For the couple, working as a team rather than as part of a triangle will enhance the love and friendship feelings that are essential to the family's well-being and to successful coping. There are a number of other guidelines that can prove beneficial to the coping process:

1. *The number-one priority should be the marriage.* Couples who are successful at working out their relationship put their relationship first. When there is a question of priorities, the needs of the couple come first. This does not mean neglecting responsibilities toward the children, but rather that there is a mutual agreement that the children's requirements can be satisfied more successfully if there is a strong marital bond. This agreement has as its basis the conviction that only a firmly committed relationship can withstand the assaults and pressures of an instant family.

2. *No one should make the mistake of marrying to provide a father or mother for his or her children.* Although the abili-

ty of a prospective spouse to relate to the children is a very important consideration, it should not be the entire basis for marriage. Again, the first priority should be to secure a marital partner. Marriages that are made for children frequently turn out to be disappointments that are hard to live with. Everybody loses in such a venture; both children and adults are deprived of the strength and warmth found in solid, loving marital relationships.

3. *The importance of parenting skills is heightened in the stepfamily.* Being at ease with children is a start, but it is not enough. The ability to prevent problems, to detect existing problems early, to solve problems reasonably is an asset. It is particularly important for one who has not parented before to become knowledgeable by reading some of the available manuals on the subject.

4. *One of the most beneficial things parents can do for their children is to stay alert to what is happening in the family.* A major part of this process involves monitoring their own feelings. Spouses would be wise to stop regularly and take stock of how they feel when they are close to the children. If they find over and over that they feel anger and tension or any other negative emotions when they interact with or about them, they should regard this as a clear signal that something is wrong.

5. *Issues involving the children that are fought and refought but resist resolution despite compromise should be reconsidered.* The conflict may not be about the children at all. Their presence, though, provides convenient camouflage. A couple might ask, "What if the children were not the issue? Would another issue surface?" If so, discuss it and see where it leads.

Children who offer themselves as buffers in marital disagreement are making an unspoken plea: "I want you to stop arguing because you are making me anxious and afraid." Sometimes, especially if they have witnessed excessive discord in a previous marriage, they feel themselves to be the cause of parental conflict. Given these fears, some parents react by hiding marital conflicts and erecting an "all is well" façade. Agreeing not to argue in front of the children is a poor solution, not only because it is virtually impossible to deny or hide all disagreement, but because an open discussion, even if heated, is of potential benefit to both parents and children. Parental dissension in which both partners air their views provides an opportunity for resolution and helps children to develop realistic expectations of what a relationship entails.

Of course, parental arguments about highly sensitive issues may be inappropriate for young witnesses and would best be held privately. Children who have been exposed to more than their share of underhanded, crude fights in which the objective is to hurt the "adversary" also need to be sheltered from more of the same. The continuance of destructive interactions is likely to increase the child's role as buffer, perhaps to the point where he will develop "symptoms" that require psychotherapeutic intervention. In these instances, the entire family should consider therapy as a group.

It may come down to this: Even under the best of circumstances, conflict and disruption are inevitable in a reconstituted family. But when husband and wife respect each other and are open about their feelings, conflict is not likely to be damaging—just difficult. Add to this a basic knowledge about parenting, a willingness to seek outside consultation when necessary, and conflict may turn into an adventure from which all family members can profit.

# 7 Stepparenting

## The Neglected Many

Stepparents are the most neglected parents in America. Our society has become very attentive to the problems of formerly married adults, but acts as if stepparents do not exist. The divorced are encouraged to find new mates, but where are the guidelines for getting along with stepchildren? Books on parenting contain very little pertaining to the special concerns of stepparents. Even in Dr. Benjamin Spock's newly revised comprehensive handbook on child rearing, no mention is made of stepparents.

It is not as if stepparents are scarce—there are quite a number of them around. In the United States, one out of every three marriages is a remarriage, and in one-third of these remarriages, *both* spouses have children from a previous marriage. It is estimated that there are fifteen million children under eighteen living in stepfamilies, and an estimated twenty-five million husbands and wives are stepparents.

Ignored by professionals, stepparents—especially stepmothers—have a poor image in the popular mind. The stereotype of the cruel stepmother is built on the negative feelings children frequently have toward their new "mother." These feelings are reinforced by tales of the wicked stepmother, such as *Cinderella,* that exist in practically every culture. Thus the stepmother finds that her reputation precedes her and biases her acceptance. Her role is often made more complicated because the child sees her as having taken the father from the real mother. All the child's resentment toward the father may be projected onto the stepmother. The stepfather has fewer problems, if for no other reason than that he is usually away from the house more than the stepmother. This does not protect him completely, however. He is frequently the target of resentment because the child has lost some of the motherly attention he or she had before the remarriage.

Stepmothers probably stir up more antagonism than stepfathers because they frequently effect radical changes in the new household and spend more time with the children. Proximity and the nature of the role produce more opportunities for disharmony. The wise father, realizing this, can decrease the disharmony by actively asserting himself as a parent rather than suddenly detaching himself when his new wife comes in to "take over." When a husband fails to ease his wife into the stepparenting role, the experience can be harsh indeed. Leslie Brooks, a one-time dancer admired and respected in her profession, now a wife and stepmother, had such an experience.

"I thought all I had to do was cook and give them lots of love and they'd fall into my arms in gratitude. Neither commodity eradicated the difficulties. The children fought, constantly whined, lied, and generally drove me crazy. Every time I'd try to do something about it, their father would act as though it was me who had done something wrong. 'Take it easy,' he'd say, as if nothing were happening. I felt put upon, unappreciated. I thought of taking a trip alone—escaping, getting away, leaving my husband to take care of his own 'little darlings.' Neither he nor the children's mother ever thanked me for all the summers, vacations, and weekends I took care of the children. My husband went about his merry business when the children were around without dramatically altering his routine. Meanwhile I was in a state of shock, tense, resentful, and very frustrated.

"The worst of it was that my husband never defended me. I yearned at those times when the kids were hostile or rude to me to have him stand up and say, 'This is my wife; don't you dare treat her like that!' But he wouldn't. He also would not comment if they repeated something nasty their mother said about me. 'I can't damage their image of her,' he'd say. But what about my image? Am I to be the wicked stepmother of the fairy tales? Finally, I just stopped doing things for them. I let their father see what it was like when the 'maid' was off. That did it. Or, at least that drew his attention. Now, we're working with a counselor and my grievances are being taken seriously."

What Leslie Brooks sought from her husband, aside from physical assistance, is the critically important emotional nurturance every stepmother desires: *the clear, unequivocal support of her husband.* If this emotional support is not communicated, success as a stepmother is very likely to be impaired. Practically every stepmother who is pleased with her life has a husband who understands and appreciates her role as stepmother. He backs her up and validates her place in the family. Some stepmothers, deprived of reassurance, fear that they will lose their husband's love if they are at odds with the children: "I don't dare tell my husband about Karen's nastiness toward me; it will make him think less of me." It is as if the stepmother has granted the child power to sanction her marriage, or even more troublesome, to control it.

The way out of this predicament requires the courage to go beyond feelings of shame or failure for events that are, in fact, endemic to steprelations. Difficulties must be talked out. In second marriages, there is a greater reluctance to do this. Having experienced one failed marriage, the couple is so fearful of another that negative feelings are hidden or ignored. But they don't go away and the discontent escalates. By withholding feelings instead of talking about them, stepparents can actually bring to pass whatever it is they were trying to avoid.

While the stepmother is burdened with the myth of cruelty, the stepfather operates without myth; he has no clear-cut guidelines to follow or reputation to disprove. Rather, he is confronted with the dilemma of a role that has no form; his role is to play no role. When a man became a stepfather at the turn of the century, he moved into the new household knowing what was expected of him. In four out of five instances, he married a widow and ascended to the position of father surrogate with a minimum of ambivalence. He supported his stepchildren, disciplined them, and shared responsibility for them with nobody except their mother. Head-of-household authority was bestowed quickly; just as he knew what was expected of him, so did everybody else.

Today, most men become stepfathers through divorce, not death. Frequently, the stepfather is a stand-in to children whose biological father supports them, has convictions about their upbringing, and may see them fairly regularly, at least for a while. For these reasons, today's stepfather is likely to have an undefined relationship with his children. In the beginning, neither he nor they will be clear about what to expect from one another:

"Ever since we were married, I tried to develop some parameters to erect a structure for my role in the family. It was very frustrating. There was a mother-child power bloc. I felt that my wife and Freddy, my stepson, had expectations about my role, but they didn't give me a clear picture of these expectations. I didn't know what I had been cast as, but when I didn't measure up, I was quickly branded as unsatisfactory—particularly by my stepson.

"During Christmas vacation, Freddy, his mother, and I visited their hometown. I met Freddy's father there for the first time. I was really taken by the resemblance between Freddy and his father—not only physically, but in personality. Both he and his father had an easygoing, take-life-as-it-comes manner—something that I lacked and had long envied in other people. In addition to the resemblance, I was unprepared for Freddy's response to his father. I found myself resenting his show of affection for a father who sends written instructions as to his upbringing but who never comes to see him—we have to ship Freddy off there every few months.

"By the time we arrived back home, I was feeling uptight about my function with Freddy. I didn't know where I stood. I found myself becoming much more critical and demanding of him. I kept a tighter rein on him, disciplining him often—too often, actually—and at the same time I expected him to take more responsibility for himself. I complained to my wife that we had been babying Freddy too much, that we were not building self-reliance in him. At the same time, I contradicted myself by constantly harping on the kid. Funny, I was so enmeshed in this whole thing that it wasn't until several weeks later in a conversation with a friend, also a stepfather, that I realized my ambivalence about my role, and my feeling of being threatened by Freddy's father, had influenced me to overreact."

The ambiguity of the stepfather's role can be problematic, but it also offers an opportunity. To a considerable extent, today's stepfather can make his parenting function whatever he wants it to be. Indeed, one of the reasons stepfathers seem to have an easier time of it than stepmothers may be that in our era the role of fathers in general is more flexible and less well defined than that of mothers. Unless she has a job that takes her away from home, every child has fixed expectations for Mother: She takes care of the children, runs the house, cooks, shops, and checks the homework. The average child does not have as fixed and rigid a conception of his father's function. Thus stepfathers have a freedom to develop their own fathering style.

In this regard, Dr. Paul Bohannon, an anthropologist who has studied large numbers of families headed by stepfathers, reports in a January 1978 *Psychology Today* article, "Stepping In," that fathers, including stepfathers, can provide different types of parenting experiences, falling roughly into four categories: Instrumental, Expressive, Autocratic, and Patriarchal. The Instrumental Father is one who sees his major role as that of a breadwinner and who spends little time with his family. The Expressive Father is concerned with the emotional aspects of family life and feels that a father should spend a lot of time with his child. The primary concern of the Autocratic Father is rule enforcement, while the Patriarchal Father is mostly concerned with providing a model of high personal competence and self-esteem for the child.

Bohannon and his fellow researchers found a high correlation between the style of fathering and a child's adjustment. The healthiest children, their data suggest, are those of Expressive Fathers. Although a preliminary finding, Dr. Bohannon's conclusion offers an important clue to successful stepfathering: Most children, despite having a biological father in the background, long for their stepfathers to take more active roles with them, do more things with them, show signs of caring about them.

Of course, taking a strong interest, expressing affection, and giving time to the children do not usually produce instant results. It is unrealistic to expect them to. Even under ideal circumstances, children need time to accept the experience of a new person.

Margaret Mead offers a possible reason for the difficulties children have in adjusting to their stepparent—whether it be mother or father. She suggests that in our family system, the child develops an overdependence on the parents. This results in a demand on the parents to supply the only possible security for the child. In her essay, "Anomolies in American Postdivorce Relationships," Dr. Mead states, "Each American child learns early and in terror that his whole security depends on that single set of parents. . . . We have never made adequate social provision for the security and identity of the children if that marriage is broken." The result, she points out, is the inability of a child to commit himself to a stepparent in a manner that will permit a meaningful relationship.

It is now over a decade since Dr. Mead's observations were published. Although evidence for her view still abounds, as children become more accustomed to seeing families reform with different marital partners, they are likely to be less terrified of having the ground pulled from under them if their parents part. They may adjust more quickly than children did a decade ago. Today they will not be the only kid in the neighborhood with two sets of parents, and they may even learn to draw out the advantages of the situation. Close ties with other members of the family—grandparents, aunts, uncles, and cousins—also ease the disruption should a marriage dissolve and a new one commence. Of even further benefit—at least eventually—is an awareness of the difficult issues challenging stepparents and a willingness to face them openly. Below is a discussion of several such issues.

## Special Considerations

### Disinterested/Disliking Stepparents

Some parents like their children a lot and some, unfortunately, do not like them very much at all. The same applies to stepparents. Feelings of liking and not liking are as important in the reconstituted family as they are in any other human encounter. There are stepparents who communicate warmth to their stepchildren and who invite closeness. There are others whose reserve of tolerance has been depleted by a difficult life, who are absorbed by their own concerns, and who find contact with their stepchildren tormenting.

The majority of stepparents are neither wildly in love with nor strongly repulsed by their instant progeny. They have mixed feelings. While stepparents who begin a marriage feeling negative or positive toward a child may maintain that stance over a long period of time, frequently shifts occur as the child passes through different stages of development and as the parents function more effectively as a team. One stepfather, for example, felt particularly irritated by what he termed the sissy behavior of his young stepson, whom he considered to be too close to his mother. In discussing this matter, the boy's mother and stepfather realized that the important issue was that she did not trust him to treat her son properly. When the parents settled their differences, the stepfather experienced an upsurge of positive, loving affection toward the boy that he had been withholding.

In another family, a stepmother felt negatively toward her stepchildren because after completing her parenting tasks each day, she was completely drained and unable to pursue any personal interests. She became considerably more positive toward them when her husband took on more parenting responsibilities and concurrently the children became less dependent, enabling her to obtain fulfillment in part-time employment. The reverse process can also occur; positive feelings can turn sour. A mother who begins with a positive attitude can become bitter and resentful toward her stepchildren if her husband throws most of the parenting and household responsibilities on her shoulders. One stepmother became so overwhelmed by the load that she began to see the children as burdens who were frustrating her life. It did not take the children long to sense her attitude, react negatively, and consequently aggravate her growing dissatisfaction with the marriage.

It is painful and distressing when a couple becomes aware that there are feelings of dislike toward the children. The stepparent is likely to react defensively, to feel guilty, villainous. The biological parent may feel resentful and hurt, and may attempt to overcompensate for the stepparent's dislike. Fueled by injured feelings, both adults ignite an emotional fire that spreads menacingly throughout the family: The parent, feeling the stepparent is ignoring or treating the child poorly, reacts by heaping increased affection on the child. The stepparent, feeling alienated, discouraged, and jealous, retaliates by further ignoring the child or by pressing him harder and continuing to diminish him. The parent counters by lavishing even more affection on the child, which leads to increased rejection by the stepparent and so on.

The destructive rejection-overcompensation cycle can be broken or at least made less distressing if parent, stepparent, and possibly even the child recognize what is taking place and discuss it openly. In an open forum, it may become evident that the problem is not so much dislike of the child as it is circumstances (e.g., overbearing responsibility) or unresolved feelings between the parents. A plan can be developed, with professional assistance if necessary, to correct the imbalance or disharmony and break the negative cycle.

If the problem is mainly dislike for or disinterest in the stepchild, the child will require emotional protection. A statement that suggests to the child that he is loved by his parent, that he has others who love him (relatives, close friends) but that does not put down the stepparent is important. The purpose of the statement, which may require occasional repetition, is not to undermine the stepparent but to reassure the child so that he won't feel personally diminished by skimpy or poor attention from his stepparent. The parents, too, can benefit from a realistic assessment: Some people are naturally nurturing and supportive—they readily understand and like children and merge with a ready-made family easily; others are not natural parents. For them, the process of a merger will be prolonged if they are pressured to feel something they do not feel.

**A Baby of Our Own**

There are many pressures to produce a child in a new marriage. Husband and wife may bring to their union similar but noncollaborative experiences: One (or both) may have been childless, unhappy parents, single parents, or noncustodial parents; now they are stepparents—singly or together. A new child represents to them a truly mutual endeavor. Untainted by a former marriage, the new child can be a celebration of happier times, a wistful attempt to make the marriage divorce-proof, something to share for all the years of struggle, an attempt to make the family a tighter unit. Probably the desire to have a new baby embodies all these motives and more. For the stepparent, the desire often burns more strongly, especially if he or she is childless. Patricia Lyman is one such person. A school psychologist ruthlessly honest with herself, she was in her late twenties when she met David, an architect in his mid-thirties whose wife had left him and their two children.

"I have a longing for a child. I feel as if one of my own would help me feel more comfortable about my stepchildren. Looming in the back of my mind, as much as I hate to admit it, is that no matter how much I give to David's children, if their mother suddenly appeared on the scene, their devotion to her would spring alive. I feel I would become dispensable, and that bothers me. David understands how I feel—we've discussed it often—but he doesn't share my desire. He already has the satisfaction of having his own children. He feels a responsibility toward his son and daughter. After the abandonment by their mother, he wants the children to know they come first in his life. Naturally, he values our relationship, but he doesn't feel that inflicting the possible competition of a new child on them will help any of us.

"Despite his strong arguments, I find it hard to live with a proscription against an enlarged family. When the children are especially bratty, it is most difficult—'These are the children I have to look after and I can't even have one of my own.' My reaction disturbs me. This is something I haven't shared with David. It's much too personal. I sometimes wonder if David is holding back also; if maybe he wants to be babied as well as his children, and would also view a new arrival as competition. . . . I realize everybody has to give up some things to make a marriage work. David has given up his need for me to be Super-Mom with his children. He wants me to give up the vision of a child of my own. For now, we're still debating. His arguments seem more logical; mine feel emotionally sound."

The arguments against having more children are, as Patricia Lyman suggests, both logical and forceful. Topping the list of practical deterrents is cost. An infant can add significantly to the strain of a household that may already be financially insecure. The need for baby sitters, restraints on freedom, and sheer physical exhaustion also enter as practical inhibitors. The emotional strain not only includes broken nights and anxiety about infant care, but runs through the entire family in the form of excitement and fear. Once excited, family members can become terrified by the twenty-four-hour relentless responsibility. Among the myriad anxieties for both parent and stepparent is the worry about being disloyal to the existing children. The children may once again feel displaced.

The problems beg to be taken seriously, yet there are sound reasons for believing that babies do make a positive contribution to a second marriage. Besides being a delight, they can reinforce to stepchildren and stepparents the importance of the new marriage and its intent to be a permanent, productive relationship. A baby can also dilute some of the isolation the childless or noncustodial stepparent experiences. He or she may feel more a part of the family rather than an outsider. These consequences, though, are a bonus only in a solid relationship. As a primary motivation in an unsatisfactory marriage or where poor steprelations exist, a new child is likely to reap destruction rather than security. As one stepparent wisely explained, "A new baby can't reverse stepparenting problems. It can, at best, only enrich what exists. When there are difficulties, seek counseling, not conception!"

## Working Stepmothers

One of the most difficult judgments a parent has to make concerns how much nurturing children need to thrive psychologically. Fathers whose work keeps them away from the house for long periods often worry about this; mothers who work, despite the growing acceptance of this practice, frequently feel uneasy about the impact of their absence on the children. Stepmothers, who as a group tend to be overly conscientious anyway, are particularly prone to feel guilty about working. Yet stepmothers' desires for outside stimulation are as legitimate and fervent as those of other women; therefore, they are often in conflict. Sometimes, the underlying feeling of guilt is escalated by the family's reaction. Mary Peltz, a forty-four-year-old divorcée with one child, married a widower with two preadolescent girls. She describes her experience:

"I decided after about six months of marriage that it was important for me to find a job. We didn't really need the money for necessities, but it would certainly come in handy for extras. No one really reacted to my decision, but when I actually found a job and started to work, the whole family was upset. The children interpreted my working to mean that I did not want to be close with them, and they began to really misbehave. This hurt me and I reacted by ignoring them and increasing my involvement at work. That was a mistake because it only angered them more and eventuated in a crisis that required a psychologist's help. It was only after my interest in work was disentangled from their feelings of rejection that things improved."

Certainly not all, nor even the majority of instances where a mother works will result in negative consequences. On the contrary, positive effects are more likely. One of the well-documented consequences is a broadening of daughters' ideas about the feminine role. In several research efforts comparing girls of working mothers with those of nonworking mothers, it has been found that girls in the former category are more oriented toward achievement, view female competence in more positive terms, consider a wider range of potential careers, and are more likely to have a positive image of their mother. Boys of working mothers also tend to develop a more realistic appraisal of the capabilities of women. In addition, if their father increases his parenting responsibility as a result of his wife's absence, boys (and girls) are likely to view him as more nurturant than is usual in many households.

Of course, positive effects, such as those described above, depend on many things. For example, if a woman feels guilty about being away from the children or burdened by too many responsibilities, this is likely to affect her and, in turn, her children's view of her. The woman who takes outside employment because she has to may be resentful and direct her anger toward the children. In contrast, the working mother who likes what she is doing is likely to be a more compassionate parent. Another important factor is the husband's view of his wife's employment. If he has a rigid concept of how a man is supposed to act and is therefore unwilling to take on extra responsibilities within the family, disharmony is predictable. On the other hand, if a husband holds a positive view of his wife's actions and shares household responsibilities with her, it is likely their relationship will profit.

Timing is also a critical issue. To expect a youngster to get used to a new stepparent, maybe a new neighborhood, and a new baby sitter or after-school center all at once is asking a lot. A wise stepparent will make changes one at a time, and gradually, whenever possible. Further, an understanding stepparent will realize that a youngster undergoing many changes may temporarily act less mature and will be prepared to be more tolerant for a time.

A final consideration is the age of the child. It is known that very young children—two or three years old or younger—need warmth, consistent handling, and stimulation in order to thrive optimally. Since, in many instances, these qualities may not be provided for adequately by a substitute caretaker, it is probably unwise to work full time until the child gets a bit older. If working is necessary, part-time employment or employment where parent and child can have contact during the day is psychologically preferable. It is important that both parents exercise very exacting standards in the choice of a parent surrogate. One caution: It is not good practice constantly to call on an older child in the family to watch a younger one. A teenage girl, for example, who is used this way is likely to feel quite resentful—"Not only has my stepmother taken my father away, but now she has restricted me from going out with my friends." Money spent for a baby sitter to enable a teenager to pursue his or her own interests is well invested in the happiness of the family.

## Myths and Realities

Unrealistic expectations set a trap into which hundreds of thousands of stepparents walk every year. Bewildered by the ambiguities of their role, floundering in the absence of custom or guidance, and wanting all too much to succeed, they are besieged by myths that mount a painful attack against their true feelings. Understanding what stepparenting is about in practical terms, knowing what it can offer and what can and cannot be expected, is apt to make disappointment and failure less likely. Below are some of the more common misguided expectations that add to the stepparent's woes.

1. *Don't expect to love your stepchildren instantly.* Occasionally people come to prefer their stepchildren to their own children; they may have a more straightforward relationship with them or find them more suitably matched in temperament and develop an instant affection. But this is rare. Too many forces act against it. A stepparent may feel he has no right to love another person's children; he may resent their intrusion, and usually they will rebel against his. None of these factors makes for positive feelings. Testing, not love, is likely to be high on everyone's agenda. Each member—for quite some time, maybe even a year or two—will have as a prime concern ascertaining his or her place in the new family structure. Not facing up to this reality causes problems. It shrouds the family in pretense.

A family can hold so tightly to the fiction that "stepparent must love the children" that any evidence to the contrary is taken as unkindness or even cruelty. It is not long before the stepparent begins to feel like the "watched parent," a term Brenda Maddox uses in her book *The Half-Parent.* "Stepparents," she writes, "feel that the world is watching to see if they will be cruel. They feel that their finest motives may be misinterpreted. In anticipation of criticism, they bend over backward to appear kind." Stepparents will find bending over backward breaks more than vertebrae; such emotional acrobatics have dangers for them, stepchild, and spouse.

2. *Don't expect your stepchildren to love you instantly.* In the original family, the children see their mother and father as a combined force, two people who often respond as one. With the loss of a parent, the children come to depend entirely on the remaining adult, sometimes for a period of years. It is very difficult for them to shift their loyalty upon that parent's remarriage. The stepparent will not only be deprived of their

love, but may even be excluded from decisions and conversations. Children often ask favors ("Can I have money for ice cream?") of their parent and converse ("Hey, Mom, guess what I did today?") as if their stepparent were nonexistent.

Stepparents who pressure themselves—or defer to pressures from their mate ("love me, love my child")—to feel something they do not feel become distraught. They will also be disappointed if they demand love be shown them. As harsh as it sounds, no matter how great the effort, neither the stepparent nor the child may ever achieve the kind of love that biological parents and their offspring often experience. This is not to say that warm, loving feelings cannot exist between steprelations, but they will probably not exist with the same intensity found in comparable biological relations. Moreover, trying too hard to create intense love feelings is likely to backfire.

Roberta, a twenty-year-old woman whose mother remarried when she was eleven, says it well:

"I now see that Marvin was really a good man with the best of intentions, but he was so terribly insecure. For example, from the start I could never talk to my mother when he was in the room because he would constantly dominate the conversation. Or, when my mother and I would be alone for a few minutes, it was like he got nervous and insisted on joining us. It was like a constant, 'Oh, wait, I'll join you.' This happened so often that I felt like saying, 'Damnit, Marvin, stop crowding me. You are not my father. Can't you understand that?' Of course, I never said it. We weren't quite that open. Besides, I wouldn't have wanted to hurt him. I just wanted him to stop forcing himself on me. The pressure for immediate bonding was stifling.

"Marvin and I have since talked about this whole thing. It surprised me that he remembered. He acknowledged feeling insecure. He thought that if my mother and I were alone, we would be analyzing or discussing him. That may have been true to some extent. But I think that pushing himself in my face and my mother's constant crusading on his behalf—'Isn't Marvin great?'—just made matters worse."

Roberta's reflections demonstrate the fallacy of trying too hard to court a stepchild's affection. It doesn't work. The stepparent-child relationship, if allowed to build slowly, can become a deeply felt bond or a reliable friendship. If rushed, peaceful coexistence or an armed truce are more likely.

3. *Expect to have money hassles.* Friction over money exists in practically all marriages. In a remarriage, money matters take on special meaning by tying the memory of the past to the present. Besides regular visiting rights, money is the issue that prevents the divorced from forgetting past attachments. A new wife may resent having to work in order to ease the financial burden. Laboring is not her grievance, though; it is having to help support her husband's former wife. To aggravate her bitterness, her own former husband's support may, at best, be sporadic. A former wife, regardless of what she receives, may not consider the sum adequate. A husband, usually held responsible for the two households' finances, is caught in a squeeze; each act of giving becomes troublesome as well as generous. He is damned if he does reach into his pocket—and damned if he doesn't. The current wife resents what he pays to the former family, and the former wife resents what he gives to the present family.

As one financially burdened man explained: "Ruth has custody of her three boys, my ex-wife has custody of my two girls. Ruth and I thought we'd be saving money by marrying. After all, some of our expenses, such as rent, were diminished. But others, I had no idea. . . . What frustrates me most is the inability to get across to all five children and the adults involved that funds are not unlimited. It has become a real problem because no one wants to change their lifestyle. Nobody is willing to give anything up. Money has become like a barometer—people are using it to get a reading as to whom I favor and whom I dislike. Sometimes when I am despondent about making ends meet, I feel they are all vultures. My love for the children—all of them—becomes buried under my weighty obligations. I find that sad. Very sad."

Capping the emotional and financial difficulties of supporting two households are the unplanned expenses. The same man continues: "The unexpected things that have happened seem unbelievable—like Ruth's kids needing expensive dental care, and just recently her ex-husband had a heart attack so her child support payments have stopped. At the same time, my ex-wife is going to court to try to increase my support payments. Talk about being squeezed!"

The dictum, "Two can live as cheaply as one"—a lie in practically any circumstance—is particularly fraudulent in remarriage. Closer to reality is the "always" mandate: When children are part of a remarriage, there are *always* more expenses than one imagines there will be; children *always* need more than one realizes; prices *always* rise; and there are *always* unexpected emergencies. Remarried couples would do well to prepare for the worst and agree in advance to discuss feelings about monetary decisions as they arrive.

4. *Expect to have confused and mixed feelings about your stepparenting role.* Sorting out what works with children and what doesn't can be a frustrating task; trial and error is part of all parenting. The stepparent, however, is haunted by a question that never occurs to a biological parent: "What is this child to me?" As stepparents struggle to discover which act is progress and which is impediment, stepchildren complicate the process by their own groping for role definition.

Stepchild and stepparent have not chosen each other but are thrown together by the bond of remarriage. Without a shared heritage, and perhaps with different values, they venture into uncertain terrain where there are no rules, no predetermined formulas. It takes time—weeks of cautious circling, months of confusion—before the fog slowly clears. To wish otherwise is human, but the wish is destined for frustration.

# Keeping the Marital Relationship Strong    8

## A Damage Report: Missed Signals

"Our marriage started out well enough; we both shared a sense of warmth, a feeling of being loved, a feeling of having taken out an option on a partnership. But as open and emotional as he was in the beginning of our relationship, just so shut in and frozen did he become over the years. Little by little he bottled up his feelings—both of love and hate—until he seemed to feel nothing at all. It disturbed the hell out of me. I found myself beginning to wonder about his complaints that his former wife had withheld love from him. Maybe by withdrawing into hurt silence every time there was a conflict, he had shut her out more often than she had shut him out. I couldn't understand why this was happening to us. In fact, I could scarcely believe it. Our sense of each other, the companionship, had been superb when we first met, and it stayed that way for some time. Then somehow he always seemed to be working late or we'd be alone for the evening but he'd drink too much and promptly fall asleep. After a while, conversation just about dried up.

"The ironic thing about this is that my friends who knew us

in the early days of our relationship would always rib us about our nonstop talking. They would comment that going out with us felt like an intrusion—we were so enraptured in our own conversation that they hated to interrupt. The climate sure changed. If we disagreed about anything, he'd get that tight, closed-up look, while I'd get loud and heated. The more withdrawn he became, the angrier I became, and the more I tried to get through to him, the more he withdrew. Anything could do it—even something as minor as planning an evening out. It would wind up with his telling me I was pushing him around and trying to control him and my telling him that he only pretended to want a woman who was together, that what he really wanted was a nice, passive, child-woman who wouldn't bruise his fragile ego. That usually resulted in a threat to knock my head off or, on a couple of occasions, a real attempt. In any case, after one of these episodes he would make himself very scarce for days on end.

"We had a final fight where he said that he married less out of love than out of a need to justify his broken marriage. He called me a 'rebound bride' and I yelled that he was a loser from the day he was born. It was so awful that he moved out that evening and came back only once to pack his things and to talk about money and other practical matters. I wanted to talk about the two of us, to see whether there was any hope at all, anything we could do, but he never let the discussion get around to that. So I choked back my tears and acted very calm as he left. He was gone, just like that. He moved to New York. During the next few months, we exchanged a few letters and spoke on the phone; we both experienced moments of longing for each other but hopes of capturing what we had had waned during the separation. We almost made it work—the start was hopeful—and we might have succeeded if we had been more skillful in ironing out our differences. If he had tackled his tendency to withdraw from contention with a woman and if I had tempered my compulsion to challenge, to blame, to feel that if I am not outspoken, a man will try to destroy me. . . ."

## Keeping the Relationship Strong

There are many reasons for marital breakup whether it be the first, second, or third time around. Some accounts are easy to explain, although usually hard to accept. Included here are instances where a man and woman grow in different, conflicting directions, or one doesn't grow up. Though differing rates of maturity are less likely in remarriage because the people are generally older, they do occur. Part of what makes a marriage work or fail lies within each person—our unique way of perceiving others. Success can also be attributed to positive combinations that two people create. Some factors, such as the chemistry of attraction, defy analysis. Occasionally circumstance—financial setbacks, for example—erodes the union beyond repair. Some second marriages collapse because too many children are undermining the relationship.

Whatever the forces operating—and usually they are a complex mixture of negative and positive—relationships do not suddenly collapse. The man and woman discussed above, both of whom thought they had it made, failed or refused to react to the signals—the subtle ones as well as the obvious ones—until their relationship had seriously deteriorated. Hurt feelings that are not rectified; thoughts (she's too domineering; he's too passive) that are not voiced; plans for renewal that are not actualized; communication that becomes a weapon—all these slowly destroy marital harmony. The disintegration occurs gradually, incrementally; once started, it grows and grows. Those couples who hold the attitude that the marital relationship will prosper by itself are mistaken; they are most vulnerable to the deterioration process. Marriage, involving two complex and ever-changing adults and, in most instances, one or more equally complex and rapidly changing children, is a difficult arrangement. Marriage will only work if both husband and wife work at it. Unfortunately, many couples do not do this; the result is a relationship filled with discord and bitterness.

Strengthening a marriage, taking steps to work as a team, is not easy. Even with the support and direction of a well-trained psychological-service provider, considerable time and effort are usually required to achieve a desired result. Patience, the courage to change, and most of all, the desire to grow are key ingredients. Given these factors, the "do it yourself" material that follows will not guarantee a perfect marriage but will provide guidelines for a workable, reasonably satisfying one. Specifically, if the suggestions are studied and seriously applied, several things are likely to occur:

1. Old destructive patterns of relating will not be so frequently activated.
2. Differences will more often be resolved without one or both partners being hurt.
3. Small problems will not become big problems as often.
4. Certain sensitive areas of the relationship will be explored more satisfactorily than previously.

## Avoiding Old Patterns: Blaming Signals

For months and sometimes years after the end of a failed marriage, the events leading to its breakdown are likely to occupy the thoughts of both man and woman. We humans are by nature unhappy with uncertainty and ambiguity. We want definitive answers; sometimes we seek simplistic solutions to complex issues. At base, in marital disputes, we want the question answered: Who's at fault? Who's to blame? This tendency, aggravated by the divorce process, unfortunately does not automatically disappear with a new commitment. In a faltering marriage, this preoccupation with mutual recrimination strikes with severe potency and frequently tips the balance in favor of separation. In a new relationship, blaming and fault-finding at the very least greatly diminish the possibility of a constructive solution to marital differences. Witness the futility of the following exchange:

SHE: You're late.
HE: I know, I tried my best.
SHE: Oh bull! It's just like you to be inconsiderate. Like father like son.
HE: *(angered)* What the hell does my father have to do with this?
SHE: *(angered but controlled)* I've seen how he treats your mother: He's late for dinner; he leaves his clothes around; he expects to be catered to. You're the same damn way and I won't stand for it!
HE: *(getting louder)* You don't say! Who's picking whose dirty underwear off the floor every morning?
SHE: That's a damn lie!
HE: Lie, my ass! You're lazy and you know it.
SHE: *(sarcastic)* Sure, sure. Keep it up. And what important events occupy you all day, genius?
HE: I happen to go to work. What have you got to do all day?
SHE: *(shouting)* I'm trying to get along on the money you don't make, that's what—Mr. Junior Junior Executive.
HE: *(walking toward the door)* Why should I knock myself out for an ungrateful bitch like you?

Quarrelsome couples expend much of their energy reviewing the last fight and preparing for the next. The mutual support system that a close attachment such as marriage can offer breaks down. For example, in a more functional relationship, one spouse might try to assuage the other's worry about the development of a noncustodial child by saying, "I think your son will be all right. Maybe we can arrange to have him spend more time with us if you think that would be helpful." In marriages in which the husband and wife are into blaming—where there are scores to settle—the expression of worry is taken as an opportunity to attack: "Can't you trust anybody to turn out all right? Can't you trust your own son?"

Typically, in the blame-counterblame trap, the angry exchanges are intended to diminish each partner's status. Motivated by the desire to reduce the spouse's capacity to hurt, each tries to deflate the other. And so the husband may become critical of the wife's housekeeping, her appearance, intelligence, sexuality, mothering, the manner in which she spends her day, her friendships, and so on. The wife may bicker about the husband's role as a father, provider, companion, his sloppy habits, his inattentiveness. Each focuses on the other's frailties illegitimately; the effort is not directed toward mutual resolution but expresses the attitude: "I'm not responsible for our difficulties; you are." From this follows: "If you are responsible for my (our) discomfort, distress, or unhappiness, only you can alter it."

Since much of the bickering is self-serving (he (she) is at fault, so *I* don't have to change), and is not really a valid attempt to solve problems, complaints are usually issued *after* the unwanted behavior, not while it is occurring. A husband may accuse his wife of being inconsiderate because she repeatedly interrupts him. He will nag, complain, sulk, and admonish—but rarely will he take a firm stand while the behavior is taking place. What if he stated while being interrupted, "You're talking over me, Barbara. Please let me finish what I'm saying." If this didn't work, he might simply get up and leave the room, saying, "It seems, by your constant interruptions, that you are not interested in what I'm saying. When you feel more like listening, let me know." Although this approach may seem severe, it is consistent and certainly discourages unwanted behavior.

Bill married while still in college and had to drop out in his third year when his wife, Jane, unexpectedly became pregnant. He gave up his dream of going to law school and went to work for an insurance company to support his family. He has since divorced Jane and now blames his second wife for his job dissatisfaction, for his lost dream, and has turned their life into a disaster by constantly criticizing everything she does. Bill feels that the responsibility of two families removes him still further from his legal ambitions. As a result of his resentment, he often sulks or explodes and tells his second wife that she makes him

**Keeping the Relationship Strong** 137

furious; consequently, minor episodes escalate into destructive fights or mutual withdrawal.

Bill has been blaming and antagonizing his wife almost constantly. If he would take responsibility for what he wants—emotional and financial support from his wife so that he could return to school on a part-time basis—instead of merely complaining, a major stumbling block to a satisfying marriage would be removed. He might immediately stop his blaming statements, express his desire for assistance to his wife, and register for one college course—taking a first step toward realizing his dreams.

Here are some additional pointers for constructive resolutions of marital gripes:

1. *Most important, fair fighting—that is fighting in which both partners are honestly striving to resolve a conflict rather than destroy or demean an "opponent"—should be the goal.* A couple can tell if they fight poorly by the results—one or both partners are constantly hurt and conflicts are hardly ever resolved.

2. *Know what the dispute is about.* When one or both partners are chronically angry and the anger is not defused as a result of discussion, this is a signal that they may be banging away at the wrong issues. For instance, sometimes trivial annoyances become decoys to evade a more burning issue, thereby leaving relationship-eroding problems unsettled.

3. *Keep the dispute focused on current issues rather than on the past.* One common unfair tactic is to dredge up the past, using yesterday's failures as today's ammunition. Both men and women are guilty of nursing past grievances and resurrecting them in the heat of battle. This is a self-defeating maneuver that results in an exchange of venomous invectives and increased hostility.

4. *Keep the communicaton empathic.* Empathy is made up of two main factors. One is listening and attempting to understand another's view rather than busily preparing a rebuttal.

The second is communicating this understanding to the speaker. A brief exercise that frequently helps to develop this pattern of communicating is "role reversal." In this exercise, when a discussion involving differences or personal/emotional issues occurs, it becomes the responsibility of the "listener" to state the partner's position and feelings until he is satisfied with the degree of understanding. If he is not satisfied with the level of understanding, a brief time-out is called while his position and related feelings are expressed again. The discussion does not proceed until each partner is satisfied that the salient aspects of his position are understood.

If a husband and wife conscientiously perform the role-reversal exercise during arguments even though it may seem forced and silly at the beginning, many difficulties caused not by actual differences, but by misunderstanding and emotional alienation will be prevented. What is more, when individuals in a dispute realize that they are being understood, that their mate sees how the situation seems to them, their statements are likely to grow less exaggerated and defensive; they will no longer find it necessary to maintain the attitude, "I am one hundred percent right and you are one hundred percent wrong."

5. *Consider compromising to resolve differences.* Whenever conflicts occur, whether between spouses, business partners, or nations, they are resolved in one of three ways: One party attempts domination (result: hostility, war); mutual or unilateral withdrawal (result: divorce, isolation); mutual compromise (result: something for something). If a couple is seeking a more satisfying relationship with each other rather than divorce or aggression, compromise clearly offers the greatest promise.

6. *Do not equate not getting your way in a dispute with a loss of self-esteem.* "Winning" or "losing" in anything has nothing to do with self-esteem. There are no magical transformations; we are the same person, with the same assets and qualities, before a dispute as after—regardless of the outcome.

## Mixed Signals

"We live in the same house, sleep in the same bed, and share a similar living routine, and yet I don't feel I really know him—there isn't a feeling of closeness between us. . . ."

"She's on the couch with her book and I'm on the chair with the newspaper; the television is going and we're both off in our own little world. We might as well be living on different continents; we never talk anymore."

These are familiar complaints to those who have suffered a broken marriage. Husbands and wives who don't talk, don't express their feelings, ideas, and viewpoints clearly, lose contact; they often feel unappreciated, alone, unhappy. Frequently, they are resentful about their unhappiness. In practically all instances, the difficulty is not a lack of communication but an exchange of messages that are confusing and misunderstood. Even if an individual turns away or is silent, a message is sent. The way a person moves, the raising of eyebrows, a frown, a surly grumble, a touch, a tone of voice—all transmit a message. So communication is constant, but it is often difficult to express oneself so that the message sent is the message received. Indeed, faulty communication is one of the major reasons for the breakdown of an otherwise workable marriage.

In troubled relationships, indirectness and confusion characterize the communication patterns. What happens is that the couple do not exchange clear, useful information. Instead, they frustrate each other with messages that appear to mean one thing but in effect convey something else. Typically, husbands and wives behaving this way believe that they know a lot more about each other than they do. A case in point: If Rose appears sullen whenever she is angry at her husband, he will soon recognize the connection. But suppose she also acts sullen for other reasons? His immediate defensive behavior (believing she is angry at him) may provoke her to anger, which then convinces him that indeed she was angry. People who assume they understand what their mates mean by certain actions, or feel in certain situations, or intend by various words or gestures or tones of voice are frequently wrong. Acting on the erroneous assumption will often trigger a mate to respond negatively, thus reaffirming the "mind reader's" conviction that he was "right in the first place."

Sid and Meryl, married three years, illustrate an exchange of information that accomplishes a further muddying of already swirling communicative waters. When Sid was still married to his first wife, he had an affair with Meryl, who was divorced. Although they enjoyed each other's company and saw each other whenever Sid was in town on business, neither thought seriously about the relationship because Sid was married. Several months later, however, Sid called Meryl to tell her that his wife had left him for another man. He then packed his belongings and within a short while transferred his business office closer to Meryl's home. During the ensuing ten months, Sid and Meryl developed their relationship and were married. Because he slept with her while he was still married to his first wife, Meryl worries that Sid will repeat this behavior. She is secretly suspicious of him and feels, occasionally, that if given the opportunity, Sid will be unfaithful to her. Sid regards his action in his previous marriage as motivated by extraordinary circumstances. His marriage had been deteriorating for a long time, his wife had refused to go for professional help, and he felt bereft, desperate. In his present relationship, he operates from a standpoint of trust and fidelity. Meryl, on the other hand, is guided by mistrust and her suspicious attitude—"If he did it to his previous wife, he will probably do it to me." Consequently, their discussions about leaves from home, particularly business trips, are fraught with conflict:

MERYL: I've been thinking, there really isn't any reason I can't get away for a few days—I'll go to the Coast with you. Maybe I can be of some help to you there.

SID: That's nice of you, Meryl, but everything is all prearranged and I'm not expecting any difficulty on this trip at all. I really don't need help.

MERYL: You know, we haven't had much time to ourselves lately. I'll come along and keep you company. The trip will give us a chance to combine work and pleasure. You can even write off my expense as business.

SID: *(experiencing a vague sense of uneasiness)* That wouldn't work out. I'm going to be tied up from early morning until very late every evening with conferences, negotiations, business dinners, and so on. We would hardly see each other—it would be more frustrating than anything else. Besides, very frankly, you would slow my pace. There's too much tension in these things for me to make accommodations.

MERYL: *(persistent, annoyed)* Since when do I slow you down! I can keep up with you anytime. I want to go!

SID: *(puzzled and antagonized)* Listen, besides the pace of things, the company won't pay your way and we really can't afford to throw money out for nothing. I won't be able to spend time with you. Can't you understand that!

MERYL: Look, Sid, it's my money, too. I'm going!

SID: *(angry and frustrated)* What in hell is going on, Meryl? When you get like this, I can't stand it. You're acting like a total stranger.

MERYL: *(her anxiety and resentment on the rise)* Stranger? I'm not acting like a stranger. What you mean is I'm acting like your ex-wife! And you, you're acting like her husband! You're bored with me. You're the one who's strange!

If communication is to be reasonably effective, untested assumptions such as Meryl and Sid's need to be clarified. By directly expressing our feelings, we enable our partner to respond to our specific assertions. We can then check our "realtiy" against the other person's response. In this instance, Sid assumed Meryl was merely being stubborn: "She can really be a baby." Meryl, of course, assumed Sid was being purposely evasive: "He doesn't want me to cramp his style with the ladies." Had she directly stated her concern or had Sid asked why the trip was so important to her, the outcome might have been quite different. Left unresolved, significant problems such as Sid and Meryl's do not go away; on the contrary, like a spreading infection, they get worse. The cycle begins with a seemingly innocent statement that quickly flares into an argument, the source of which seems clear to each but nonetheless is hidden. The result, after many futile bouts, is often you-hurt-me-so-I'll-hurt-you, and vindictiveness may become the major force in the gradual weakening of the relationship.

It is likely that a great many misunderstood communications pass between husbands and wives and that each destructive communication will lead to others. That is, as I reported in *The Other Man, The Other Woman,* once a negative, destructive atmosphere of misunderstanding is established, more indirectness and misunderstanding are probable as protection against the "enemy." For example, Meryl may begin to attack Sid on any number of insignificant issues—his dress, his manners, his punctuality, and so on. In actuality, Meryl's disturbance is related to something entirely different—she is insecure and afraid of losing Sid. Stating her real concern in the battleground atmosphere that has developed, however, would be too painful. Instead, she remains in the war zone through her relationship-defeating attempts to allay her anxiety and keep Sid off balance.

A certain amount of misunderstanding is unavoidable in any relationship. But attempts at promoting guilt and anxiety in one's partner—coaxing, manipulating, threatening, mind reading, and veiled statements—will only promote confusion and discord. "There's a new movie down the street," Muriel says to Arnold. This is a vague statement that sounds more like an observation than a request. A more direct, functional statement would be, "I would like to see a movie with you." Another seemingly innocent observation that in fact camouflages an underlying statement: "Phil told me he and his wife have sex almost every night." Rather than stating directly, "I am not satisfied with our sex life," and discussing the issue, the intent here is to promote guilt and thereby motivate the partner to greater sexuality. The result is much more likely to be resentment.

A couple has just come out of the water after a delightful moonlight swim. The woman says, "Let's go inside, I'm sleepy." The man responds, "It's nice out here. Why don't we lie and rest here." The woman, angry, storms into the house. The man, equally angry, drives off to a local bar. What happened? She, by saying she was "sleepy," was actually signaling her desire to make love in the house. He, ironically, was signaling his desire to make love in the moonlight. Neither said what he or she wanted directly. Both felt rejected and the evening ended in anger and hurt rather than pleasure. Preventing this unfortunate turn of events may have been as simple as saying, "Let's go inside, I'm in the mood to make love," or "It's nice out here, why don't we make love in the moonlight?"

When something is wanted, be it change, clarification, reassurance, companionship, or support, it is important that the message be direct and to the point. Speaking in generalities, dropping "cute" hints, expecting your spouse to guess your intent, won't get the job done.

## Sex and Intimacy: Connecting the Signals

The German philosopher Schopenhauer told the story of two porcupines huddled together on a cold winter's night. The temperature dropped; the animals moved closer together. But then there was a problem: Each kept getting "stuck" by the other's quills. Finally, with much shifting and shuffling positions, they managed to work out an equilibrium whereby each got maximum warmth with a minimum of painful pricking from the other. Many husbands and wives are like the huddling porcupines. They want to achieve and maintain warmth and intimacy without the sometimes agonizing friction that comes from continuous interaction with another human being.

Invariably, sex—invested with an exaggerated importance by our culture—enters the intimacy arena. Of the many forms of intimacy—a smile across a room, a shared hardship, a family ritual, a kiss, a touch—sex is probably fraught with more confusion, unrealistic expectations, misunderstanding, and disillusionment than any other. For many of the remarried—both men and women—the pressure to perform sexually adds a burdensome demand to their bond. The emphasis on sexual technique, on being a "super" lover—a frantic effort to make up for past dissatisfaction—cuts off many couples from true intimacy. Caught up in the mechanics and methods of satisfying their partner, they lose sight of the most basic aspect of sexuality: the expression of feelings. A case in point involves the experience of Joan and Martin Wyden, both married for the second time.

Joan Wyden:

"My former husband was a good provider, a good father—and a lousy partner. He never expressed any appreciation for me and rarely even kissed me. It was sex and no closeness. After a few years of the same nonaffectionate routine, our sex was contaminated; it became a weapon in a power struggle. If I couldn't get him to respond to me as a person, to be tender and loving, I wasn't going to respond to him physically and emotionally. I started withholding sex or giving it and going through the motions in a perfunctory manner. I was saying directly and through sex: 'I want our relationship to be better—warmer, more feeling-oriented, less mechanical.' He was either threatened by that or he misunderstood or something, because he became very rigid and countered with, 'You're frigid; you have sexual hang-ups.' That was his favorite line. In my view, our sexual problems were really relationship problems that expressed themselves sexually. I think sex enjoyment is increased by how we act toward each other in all aspects of our lives together. Sex is part of the relationship; I don't see it as a separate entity."

Martin Wyden:

"I agree with Joan. I feel sex is an integral part of a relationship. That's what makes it so gratifying. When we were first married, I went through a few months of fear about how good she would think my performance was and how I compared to other lovers—I was particularly plagued by imagined comparisons to her former husband: 'Was she matching our abilities as lovers? Did I measure up to him in that regard?' I also came into the situation with a backlog of negative reactions from my first wife. Maybe in some marriages the sex stays good even if the relationship doesn't. Not in mine. Sex became terrible and we both traded barbs in that area. So sex with Joan—an important person in my life—was tense. I was giving myself a hard time from several quarters.

"One night something interesting happened that has had a very positive effect. Joan was feeling sexier than I and she came on to me. I had had a particularly grueling day and really wasn't in the mood for sex but she snuggled up to me and I felt compelled to respond. Things didn't go too well, though. I couldn't get aroused; I wasn't able to get an erection. So I said to Joan, 'I'm sorry,' She looked at me with love and tenderness and said, 'Don't be sorry. You don't have to prove anything to me. I love you next to me, holding me, talking to me. You can touch me, kiss me, I love it! Our relationship is not going to be judged by erections!' From that time on, my performance fears have disappeared. Joan was right. Two people who are basically loving toward each other, who experience goodwill toward each other, don't need to prove through sex that they're valuable people. All we have to do is relax and enjoy each other."

While sex can be the peak physical experience of intimacy, there are any number of ways every couple can find to enhance and express their mutual feelings of closeness:

1. *One of the greatest conflicts in marital intimacy is based on a simple truth: There are times when we want intimacy with our spouse and there are times when we want to be alone or with someone else.* We all know this, but many of us find it difficult to accept—particularly when we want our husband or wife to be with us. This refusal to accept another person as an

individual free to see personal friends or pursue independent interests will reflect poorly on intimacy. Living a rich life with another person requires time to talk and to be quiet, time to play together and to work side by side, time for sex, time to be spouse, parent, and lover, but also time to be separate.

2. *Self-disclosure is an important aspect of intimacy.* Think back and ask yourself whether you often tell a friend or neighbor something you feel you can't or do not want to tell your wife or husband. If you do, perhaps you should ask whether you are being emotionally fair to your partner. Do you fear that your mate will take advantage of your disclosure? Relationships in which self-disclosure is minimized are lacking in trust. If trust is not increased, it is unrealistic to expect greater intimacy.

3. *Trust is one of the necessary ingredients for true intimacy.* The exchange of trust encourages spouses to be generous, consoling, and comforting. Trust is developed as a couple practices honesty in communication; it requires a mutually shared risk by spouses to be truthful and open about themselves. For example, if a husband can admit he is afraid that he is failing at his job instead of attacking his wife for spending too much money, support and helpfulness are possible. Tolerance and generosity become easier when an individual openly acknowledges his fallibility. Similarly, if a person is courageous and honest enough to admit his mistakes—and finds he is forgiven—it then becomes possible for him to be tolerant of his mate's (or other people's) foibles.

4. *Many men and women find pleasure in varying degrees of physical intimacy short of full sexual contact.* Touching is one such contact. Unfortunately, some people think of touching not in terms of comfort and affection but in terms of sex or aggression. Thus a wife may come to resent a husband's touch because she regards it as a signal for sex: "He only touches me when he wants to sleep with me." Just as she is suspicious of his touch, she hesitates to touch him for fear he will think she wants

sex. Couples caught in this obstacle to intimacy might first discuss the issue and then begin increasing contact through touching. A couple can greatly enhance intimacy—both sexual and nonsexual—by learning to be sensitive to their partner's desire (or lack of desire) to be touched.

5. *Just as there are many kinds of sex—emotional mergings, casual lovemaking, playful seduction, tension-release coupling, and very physical, lusty contacts—intimate behavior does not have to involve only grand passion.* Intimacy can be expressed by less dramatic gestures: giving a small but unexpected present; expressing an appreciation; doing a favor; being sensitive; telling the other person something positive about him or her.

## Silent Signals

The signals flashed between a couple—whether they are angry, sexy, intimate, missed, or mixed—are often at least partially nonverbal. Analysis of slow-motion films of couples in various situations reveals that the two individuals continually "speak" to each other in nonverbal modes (gestures, actions, facial expressions, and the like). The most profound form of nonverbal communication is, of course, sex. But the ways in which your mate walks, stands, holds her head, makes (or avoids) eye contact, smiles, or frowns are also important—often these cues tell you far more than words.

Most interchanges between a husband and wife provide a sensory cue that enriches the verbal report. For example, if a husband suggests sex to his wife and she says no, the meaning of her response can be clarified by the facial expression that accompanies it. If, as she says no, she smiles, she may be signaling: "Don't just ask; seduce me; be playful." If she frowns and presses her lips together angrily, her refusal is scornful and decisive: "I'm angry; how can you expect me to be intimate after embarrassing me last night!" If she offers a meek no, exhaling emphatically as she responds, her decline may be more delay than refusal: "I'm pretty tired now, but perhaps later—or tomorrow." In each instance, the same verbal response was given but the unspoken accompaniment relayed a very different message.

We tend to ignore many silent signals, particularly in our marital relationships. In many cases, we simply become so used to our mate's nonverbal signs that they cease to affect us on a conscious level. Sometimes, too, we deliberately screen them out or disregard them either from impatience or because we misunderstand their intent. Consider the following exchange:

The scene takes place around midnight at a house party. Gail Blythe is tired and eager to return home; her six-year-old has been ill and she was up several times the previous night comforting him. Gail's husband, David, is seated next to a young attractive woman and is heavily engrossed in conversation. Gail positions herself so that she is able to make eye contact with David and then taps her foot impatiently while motioning toward the door with her head.

DAVID: *(to himself)* She's jealous; she wants me to leave. David's temporary companion, Gloria, also recognizes the message.
GLORIA: *(to herself)* His wife wants him to leave. Let's see what kind of choice he makes.

With this unspoken challenge, Gloria leans toward David, tosses her head back, letting her hair fall freely in a provocative manner.

DAVID: *(turns his back to his wife and thinks to himself)* She's not going to order me around.
GAIL: *(to herself)* What a selfish bastard! He knows I'm tired; wait until we get home!

Gail and David Blythe's spat illustrates the importance of being sensitive to your mate's silent signals. In a very brief wordless exchange, a plea to leave was sent and misunderstood; feelings of jealousy were interpreted; a challenge was offered by Gloria; and David reacted as if his "manhood" were at stake. Feelings of anger, seduction, hurt, and confusion ensued.

On other occasions, it is not so much that couples misread the nonverbal cues but that the nonverbal aspect of the message contradicts the spoken word. Larry may say to his wife, "I'm listening, I'm listening," while glancing at the morning newspaper. Allen may tell his wife, "I love you," over and over but say it in a flippant manner while focusing his attention elsewhere. The partners of both Allen and Larry have good cause to wonder about the reliability of the messages they are receiving.

Whenever our verbal and nonverbal forms of communication are discrepant—when our words convey one message but our tone of voice or body another—we are likely to arouse suspicion and confusion in the listener. Sometimes the discrepancy is a signal that there is an underlying problem in the relationship. Discovering the contradictions and discussing them may well bring to awareness unrecognized feelings, gripes, and desires. Larry was obviously more interested in the morning's news than in conversing with his wife. Larry could have said, "Couldn't we wait till later, Phyllis?" If Phyllis felt strongly about talking, she could have made this known: if she didn't, she could have respected Larry's desire to delay the conversation.

Larry and Phyllis were being overly polite in an attempt to create an impression that is unreasonable: We are *always* desirous of contact with each other. In actuality, both Larry and Phyllis were collecting "resentment stamps" in regard to this issue. Many marriages are burdened with this and similar relationship-eroding demands. Most often they are evident in nonverbal behavior. Recognizing and countering the irrational premises in a marriage can be aided immensely by attention to *how* a message is conveyed as well as to the content of the message. This is not to suggest that spouses should immediately clobber each other with, "Aha, I caught you in a lie!" Instead, a frank, nonaccusatory discussion of the contradiction can be used to lead to greater openness and trust in the relationship.

## Checking the Signals: Keeping the Dialogue Alive

There is a myth in this country that the first few months of marriage form the period during which all problems "get ironed out." The implication is that people are static and that the marriage relationship is also static. Nothing could be farther from the truth. Divorce figures indicate just how fallacious this myth is. Couples who sit passively by hoping that "every day things will get better and better" are inviting disaster. Pretending that problems do not exist or that there is no room for growth is a guarantee of unhappiness.

The amount of energy required to support an unsatisfactory or poorly functioning relationship is at least equal to that required to build a workable relationship. As an aid to keep the marital dialogue alive and gainful, a questionnaire to be responded to jointly follows. The questions are intended to assist a couple in identifying and appraising marital liabilities and assets. A specific scoring system is not used; rather, the responses, given out loud in each other's presence, will serve as stimuli for continuing discussion. Responses should be given in the spirit of caring and understanding, not to put your partner on the spot. The purpose is to get close—not to drive a wedge of defensiveness between you. The questionnaire is not meant to provide an excuse for a "dumping" session where you hurt or depress each other. It is meant to give your partner new insight into some of your behavior and feelings.

## Instructions

Each spouse is to take turns at being the first to answer a question. The answers should be kept brief, with no comment made until each partner has had a chance to respond fully.

# Keeping the Relationship Strong

Comments are to be limited to clarification. This will enable a couple to go through the entire procedure in one sitting and to obtain an impression of the qualities and defects of the relationship. Preferably within one week, the couple can arrange to go over the questions again. This time each question is discussed more fully in terms of satisfaction/dissatisfaction, and solutions may be attempted using the principles of communication outlined earlier.

1. What qualities first attracted you to your husband/wife? Obviously there was a time when you had common interests, shared common goals, did things together that you both enjoyed. Are these factors still present and used constructively?

2. Describe five expectations you have regarding your marriage. Begin each of your statements with, "I expect . . ." For example, "I expect marriage to provide continuingly exciting sex." Discuss with your mate the compatibility and attainability of each other's expectations.

3. Discuss five factors you have learned from your previous marriage and the postmarital period that you put to constructive use in your present relationship.

4. Briefly describe at least one current disappointment in your marriage. What factors do you think account for this failing? What obstacles stand in the way of a positive resolution?

5. Have there been occasions when you wanted to show affection to your mate and did not? What was the basis of your restraint? Give full details.

6. Discuss an instance in which your spouse was deliberately or unwittingly hurt as a result of an argument. Review the quarrel in retrospect and discuss how it could have been handled more constructively so that it ended with an improved relationship instead of a bruised one.

7. Discuss your reactions (agreement/disagreement and why) to the following statements:

a) I believe I do more than my share to make our marriage work.

b) Though I work hard for our family in many ways, I must confess I am taken for granted more than I ought to be.

c) My spouse's caring for me seems to exert a kind of control over me; I feel smothered.

8. Do you tend to make snap judgments about the emotional significance of your spouse's remarks? For example, a wife's question—"What time will you be home tonight?"—may set up automatic resentment in a husband, who concludes: "She's checking on me again; I can't have a moment's freedom." Identify the types of statements that are emotionally provocative to each of you and attempt to clarify their intended meaning.

9. Is your sex life satisfactory to you? If not, what suggestions would you offer for improvement?

10. List five advantages or satisfactory aspects of your marriage.

11. Would you prefer more time alone? More time alone with your mate? More time spent in company? Discuss your responses and develop a plan for actualizing your preferences.

12. What are the major decisions each of you feels you make? What are the minor ones? Are you truly "in charge" of those matters about which you have a right to decide? Or has your spouse merely abdicated them or tacitly given you permission to manage them?

13. List five ways in which you'd like your mate to change. List five ways in which you'd like to change. Would

these changes please your mate? Why haven't they been implemented?

14. Do you know of a couple with a marriage better than yours? If you do know of such a couple, what factors account for the superiority of their marriage?

15. Were you happier during your courting period than you are now? If so, give at least three reasons why.

16. *For the stepparent:*
If you are not getting adequate support from your mate in this area, state, very specifically, the nature of your dissatisfaction. For example, "I would like my husband (wife) to spend more time with the children on weekday evenings."

17. *For the biological parent:*
Do you feel caught in a conflict of loyalty between your mate and your children? If so, what suggestions would you offer to your mate to reverse this negative trend?

18. What are your aspirations and expectations for your marriage in the future? Be specific: For example, "I would like parenting responsibilities to be divided more fairly;" "I would like my wife to become more affectionate;" and so on. Name at least five aspirations. Describe what you are doing to ensure that these hopes will be realized.

# 9 Getting There with Help: Marital and Family Therapy

## Considering the Need

Since the beginning of time, human beings have expended immense effort in attempts to change members of their families—to make their sons, daughters, husbands, wives, and relatives fit some idealized image. In our efforts to influence others, we have resorted to every imaginable device, from cruel, inhumane punishment to devious flattery. For the most part, these efforts have been unsuccessful; most of us resist—covertly or blatantly—the demand that we live up to others' expectations of what we "should" be. The rebellion may take many forms—overeating, infidelity, or in more extreme instances, suicide. In its active state, resistance to imposed change may result in chronic arguing, leaving home, or complete estrangement. All of us strive to maintain our own identity as a unique, independent person. To frustrate this tendency is to ask for grief. So much for coercion.

At the same time that we resist imposed change, most of us are never completely satisfied with ourselves and down through the ages we have also employed innumerable devices in our *own* efforts to change. Prophets, idols, witch doctors, priests, wise men, scholars, friends, and family have been sought out for advice on how to achieve growth. Some of these efforts have been successful. We all know of instances where loving parents, a compassionate spouse, true friends, and inspiring teachers have provided the spark that enabled persons to change the entire direction of their lives.

Major events, too, provide significant turning points in our lives. The death of a loved one, a new job, a health crisis, a major relocation, all require a shifting of gears, a new adjustment. But perhaps the most complex (and increasingly common) turning point for many people is the birth of a new marriage commitment; two adults who arrive at the marriage altar filled with a curious mix of apprehension and hope—in addition to several children of different sexes and ages and with different needs, personalities, and past experiences—are perhaps facing the ultimate in change.

How we react to this fork in the road of life is crucial, for it will influence the remainder of our days. Each event, each crisis that we handle successfully strengthens us for the journey ahead. If we do not learn from each failure, we lead ourselves farther from the main highway of rich, zestful living. In this final chapter, marital and family therapy, a resource that is being increasingly used to reach this goal, will be discussed.

## The Call for Help: Recognizing the Need

How can you identify the boundary lines that differentiate a conflict you can resolve yourselves from one that requires the guidance of a trained therapist? What are the key indications that marital or family therapy is warranted? When will "trying to work it out ourselves" result in marital impairment rather than improvement? The most important danger signals indicating that a couple should consider getting the assistance of a professional third party are these:

>  1. *The feeling by one partner that he or she is giving more than the other; that the rewards of the relationship are not worth*

*the cost.* In these circumstances, one partner may feel unable to meet the needs of the other, or a spouse may feel ignored or unwanted by the family (I'm only useful as a money-maker (maid), otherwise no one really gives a damn). In either case, there are usually feelings of loneliness and isolation associated with the relationship.

2. *The inability to move from inflexible, conflicting positions.* The couple caught in this difficulty behave as though they have a vested interest in rejecting each other's point of view; each refuses to acknowledge there could be merit to any perspective but their own. Because of their rigid belief—"I am one hundred percent right, you are one hundred percent wrong"—both husband and wife usually refuse professional intervention until one of their children develops problems as a result of their marital disturbance.

3. *Arguments that are frequent and unproductive.* This pattern involves an escalating series of violent verbal exchanges —accusations, insults, frequent criticism, recriminations, and threats to seek separation. Sometimes the provocation takes the form of arguments over what appear to be insignificant issues; other times, the children, ex-spouses, or money matters provide the spark for mutual abuse.

4. *Severe psychological problems or dramatic gestures— suicide attempts, physical violence, leaving home—that drain emotional energy that could ordinarily be directed to self-help.* Psychological problems can include alcoholism, compulsive gambling, frequent lying, chronic anxiety, and deep feelings of insecurity or inadequacy. Whenever severe problems are evident it is important that a skilled therapist be consulted. Even if the disturbed individual will not agree to therapy, the other partner would be wise to consult with a therapist so that he or she can learn to handle both the situation and his or her own pain.

5. *A lack of enjoyment and pleasure in a spouse's company.* A marriage is in trouble when you feel that you can function better without your spouse than with him. It is not working

when, after repeated attempts at self-help, you would rather be alone or with sombody else than with your partner—not sometimes but usually. Professional assistance would wisely be considered when there is no fun in the marriage.

These are some of the more common danger signals. Add to these frequent avoidance of each other, overdependence on the part of one or both partners, sexual dissatisfaction, and the list becomes comprehensive. When should you seek help? Not after a short-lived, shallow dip in domestic satisfaction. A day's arguing over the children, a few days of melancholy or acute tension —these are not necessarily signs of trouble. They are more probably results of the normal strain of living in a difficult world. The key is repetition—a *continued* feeling of resentment, loneliness, hurt, and so on.

Frequently, when a couple have experienced distress over an extended period of time, they exert a vital influence on the children. Noxious marital relationships touch everyone in the family. Consequently, it is not unusual for a child to develop symptoms:

"Our fifteen-year-old ran away from home." "Linda is failing most of her subjects in school." "Jeffrey was caught shoplifting again." "Marcia is constantly lying." "Peter has no friends and won't listen to anything we say."

In these instances, both parents and children should be seen together in family therapy. As a treatment modality, family therapy can be used to remedy problems similar to those above.

Members of reconstituted families need not wait till problems arise; short-term family therapy can be used just prior to a new marriage or during the early part of the union to prevent problems from occurring. Because mythical as well as real expectations, hopes, and fears are shared by most family members, and because they are culturally reinforced, the family therapist can make an important contribution by challenging and decreasing them. Moreover, because we are dealing with two distinct subgroups that have to learn to live together, family treatment, with its emphasis on genuine communication, often enables the family fragments to move toward greater unity.

For children, family therapy can be particularly beneficial. Therapy gives the child the opportunity to express his feelings regarding an event over which he did not have control—his parent *chose* a marital partner, he or she *became* a stepchild. Being part of the merging process of family therapy can give the child a greater sense of participation than is otherwise possible.

## Expectations: Real and Unreal

There are several important effects that can be expected from a successful therapy experience:

1. *Family members discover, often to their great surprise, that a relationship can be lived on the basis of real feelings rather than on the basis of defensive pretense.* There is a deep and comforting significance to this; to discover that feelings of shame, anger, and annoyance can be expressed and that the relationship will survive anyway is reassuring. To express tenderness, sensitivity, and fearfulness, and not be betrayed—this is deeply strengthening.

2. *Experience in therapy teaches people how to initiate and maintain real two-way communication.* To understand another person's thoughts and feelings thoroughly, with the meanings they have for that person, and to be thoroughly understood by that person in return—this is one of the most rewarding of human experiences, and one that therapy can facilitate.

3. *Family members begin to permit each other to be separate persons.* This may seem a strange statement, but lack of separateness actually drives people away from each other. Many of us are perhaps unaware of the tremendous pressure we put on our wives, our husbands, our children, to have the same feelings we have. We silently say, "If you want me to love you, then you must have the same feelings I have. If I feel your behavior is bad, you must feel so too. If I feel a certain goal is desirable, you must too."

It is also realistic to expect a therapy experience to assist couples to: develop clear communication so that the message sent is the message received; identify the behavioral patterns and attitudes that were deteriorating the relationship; take responsibility for their part of the marital disruption rather than blame the others; practice techniques designed to increase cooperative, positive behavioral patterns and decrease negative, relationship-defeating behavioral patterns; develop the ability to negotiate and create workable compromsies.

Obtaining these very substantial benefits from a therapy experience requires an awareness of unrealistic expectations. Some people expect magic, which is not possible. Many expect the therapist to be a super detective who will cleverly find the key to unlock all their problems so that they can "live happily ever after." Others would like to find a gentle, loving father or mother who will shoulder all their burdens and pave the way to future happiness and success. Still others think of therapy as some kind of psychological surgery where the therapist neatly and quickly removes the sore and painful areas of their relationship.

All these expectations increase the likelihood of dissatisfaction with the therapy experience. There are no magic pills to be dispensed, no magic wands a therapist can wave. *A passive stance*—"Therapy will make us all better"—*is an unrealistic attitude that guarantees therapeutic failure.* This is probably the most common expectation that couples bring to therapy. In actuality, therapy can only work if the participants work at it. Expecting to transfer the relationship problems to the therapist is disastrous.

## Types of Marital and Family Therapists: Background and Qualifications

There are three major classes of mental health practitioners—psychiatrists, psychologists, and social workers. There are also professionally trained marriage and family counselors who offer treatment services to the public. Since it is important to know something about the several classes of therapists in order to make a more informed choice, a brief discussion of each follows.

## Psychiatrists

All psychiatrists are physicians who have completed medical training and have obtained a medical degree (M.D.). In some states, a psychiatrist need not have completed specialized training beyond the medical degree to practice psychiatry. That is, a physician with no special training in human behavior can call himself a psychiatrist or marital and family therapist with no approval necessary from a public accrediting body. Rather than formal training in the psychology of marital and family problems or supervised experience in helping persons solve their most pressing problems through psychological means, the physician without advanced training has been primarily schooled to handle patients administratively with drugs and hospitalization and to give rudimentary psychological first aid.

Psychiatrists who have had advanced training, particularly those who have completed the requirements of the American Board of Psychiatry, have usually spent approximately three years in psychiatric residence beyond the four years in medical school and a general (medical) internship. A good part of the residency may have been at a large mental institution such as a city or state hospital. In this setting, the people with whom the psychiatrist dealt were likely to be the severely disturbed, such as schizophrenics or chronic alcoholics. Some time of the training period, usually about six months, is spent working with neurological problems (disorders caused by patholgoical abnormalities of the brain or nerves) and some time is frequently devoted to work in an outpatient clinic, where the physician sees a variety of patients with a variety of problems.

Some psychiatrists doing psychotherapy and marital therapy rely too heavily on medical methods, especially the administration of psychoactive drugs (e.g., tranquilizers). This is certainly not the rule, but it is most common among those with insufficient advanced training in individual and marital therapy. Lacking the proper experience to intervene effectively with individuals and couples seeking to resolve the (nonmedical) problems of living, the insufficiently trained psychiatrist is likely to prescribe tranquilizers in an effort to give his anxious patient something. Unfortunately, problems of living are rarely solved by tranquilizers. Drugs may temporarily ease anxiety, but if effective therapy is not pursued, self-defeating patterns are unlikely to be reversed.

Ascertaining the psychiatrist's methods of practice may be accomplished in several ways. Asking someone who has seen him in therapy may be helpful. The psychiatrist may briefly discuss his orientation in a telephone conversation. If nothing is known about the psychiatrist except that he is qualified—that he has an M.D. and has completed the requirements for the American Board of Psychiatry—an initial consultation is wise. The couple should arrange to meet the therapist together and ask about his methods and point of view. Asking pointed questions of the therapist as to his training, experience, and attitudes may seem rude or unnecessary, but it should be remembered that therapy is an important and usually expensive venture whose success depends, in large part, upon the choice of the proper therapist. Couples may have to visit two or three different psychiatrists before finding an individual with whom they both feel comfortable and confident.

To find out if a psychiatrist is board-certified, consult a volume called *The Directory of Medical Specialists* at a local library or medical school. Or write:

> The American Board of Psychiatry and Neurology
> 1603 Orrington Avenue
> Evanston, Illinois 60201

The American Board of Psychiatry and Neurology does not make referrals. These can be obtained through a local medical association.

## Psychologists

A professional psychologist is an individual who has a doctoral degree from a regionally accredited university or professional school in a program that is primarily psychological in content. The doctor's degree takes four or five years beyond the four-year college program to complete. This includes a one-year supervised internship. All states have laws regulating the practices of psychologists. In the case of psychological practice that involves service for a fee (such as marital and family therapy), appropriate registration, certification, or licensing is required. Most states forbid anyone not so registered, certified, or licensed to represent to the public any title or description of services for a fee incorporating the words "psychology," "psychological," or "psychologist."In addition to state laws, which usually require the doctorate and licensing by exam, to be listed in the *National Register of Health Service Providers in Psychology* (available in most public libraries), a psychologist must have two years of supervised experience in health services of which at least one year is postdoctoral and one year is in an organized health service training program. Because a psychologist does not have a medical degree (in psychology the doctorate is the Ph.D., Ed.D., or Psy.D.), he is not allowed to administer drugs or other forms of physical treatment, such as insulin or electric shock. If chemotherapy is deemed necessary, the psychologist will refer the patient to a medical doctor for a prescription.

All psychologists are concerned with the dynamics of personality and behavior but their training varies considerably. Although as a group psychologists have far more extensive training in principles of human behavior than the general run of psychiatrists or social workers, they may not have had specialized training in applying their knowledge to individual or marital disturbances. Some have a strong background in experimental psychology, which includes testing theories of behavior on lower animals. Others focus on industrial psychology or personnel management—fields that have little relevance to marriage and family counseling. Psychologists in the private (or agency) practice of individual and marital therapy usually have a background in the more therapy-relevant specialties of clinical or counseling psychology, but it is wise to ask the practitioner about his or her specific experience. The *National Register of Health Service Providers in Psychology* mentioned above lists the names of several thousand psychologists who have applied and met the licensure and experience requirements for inclusion. Psychologists are listed alphabetically and geographically by city and state. If this valuable resource is not available in your local library, referral information may be obtained by writing:

> The Council for the National Register of Health
> Service Providers in Psychology
> 1200 Seventeenth Street, N.W., Suite 403
> Washington, D. C. 20036
> Tel.: (202) 833-7568

Since listing in the *Register* is voluntary, some psychologists, though qualified, will not be listed. Additional referral information can be obtained through a county or state psychological association.

## Social Workers

The minimum standard for a professional social worker is a master's degree in social work (M. S. W.) earned by the completion of a rigorous two-year program of graduate study in an accredited school of social work. In addition to receiving the required classroom instruction, candidates for the degree work two or three days a week in an agency that offers counseling services, such as a psychiatric clinic, hospital, probation department, welfare department, or family counseling clinic. This internship, spread over two years, is supervised by an experienced social worker who holds the M. S. W. degree. Usually, individuals accepted into a graduate school of social work have an undergraduate degree (B. S. or B. A.) in one of the social or behavioral sciences.

Thirteen states have laws that license the practice of social work and there is national certification by the National Academy of Social Work as well as strong local and state organizations that strive to enforce professional standards. Most social agencies are sensitive to professional standards, and in only a few, such as departments of county welfare, is the term "social worker" used for individuals who do not have the M. S. W. degree. A couple desiring marital therapy would normally not be applying for this service at a welfare agency, but at a family counseling service where the professional degree is required for employment. In seeking a private practitioner, an inquiry as to whether the individual has earned the master's degree in social work from an accredited institution is warranted.

It is important to ask the social worker questions regarding his or her professional experience. One pertinent question may be, "Have you had supervised experience in marital therapy?" Typically, social work students are offered a general program during their two years of training. This includes group work, individual casework, and community organization. A few social work schools provide for specialization in one of these areas. Thus, a student interested in training in marital and family therapy may be assigned a family counseling agency for internship. Others may obtain specialized training after obtaining the graduate degree. Although social workers are frequently accorded less status by the public and by other professionals, with appropriate training, they are as qualified to do marital therapy as psychiatrists and psychologists trained in this area. It is not so much the professional title as the individual's training, experience, and personal qualities that determine a successful therapy relationship.

To check qualifications or find a nationally certified social worker, write:

> National Association of Social Workers
> 1425 H Street, N. W.
> Suite 600
> Washington, D. C. 20005
> Tel.: (202) 628-6800

## Marriage Counselors

"Marriage counselor" is a general term that can include social workers, psychologists, psychiatrists, pastoral counselors, and individuals with a master's or doctorate degree in psychology, family relations, educational psychology, guidance counseling, or theology. Many of these counselors have received neither theoretical instruction nor practical supervised experience related to marital problems. Some, however, such as those majoring in family relations or marriage counseling, have received excellent training. Perhaps an important factor in allowing those with inadequate clinical background to practice is that in most states the title "marriage counselor" is unregulated. As of 1974, only five states—California, Michigan, New Jersey, Utah, and Nevada—had specific regulations concerning marriage counseling. Although anyone can practice in this field in those states where there are no regulations, there is a national organization for accrediting and certifying practitioners:

> The American Association of Marriage and
>   Family Counselors
> 225 Yale Avenue
> Claremont, California 91711
> Tel.: (714) 621-4749

Membership in this organization of several thousand is strictly voluntary, but the qualifications for accreditation are rigorous. To become a member, a counselor must have a graduate degree in one of the behavioral sciences plus at least two years of clinical experience in marriage counseling under supervision approved by the Association. A couple contacting the AAMFC will be supplied with a list of three (or more) accredited counselors in their geographic area.

## How to Select a Therapist

There are several ways to select a therapist that are likely to result in a satisfactory experience. If your problem is not urgent, learn all you can about sources of help in your area. In some communities, leading therapists are fairly well known not only in their own neighborhoods and organizations, but to the public in general. Perhaps they give lectures, serve on public committees, or are involved in community affairs. Often, you can form at least an initial impression through this type of contact. Sometimes recommendations made by friends, physicians, and lawyers are useful. These people may be able to direct you immediately to the assistance you seek, or they may introduce you to someone who knows the mental health system well—for example, a psychological professional or someone who works in a community health agency that frequently refers people for help.

If your first attempts at using friends, relatives, and other professionals to find proper help do not provide enough information, try more formal methods. For example, the following sources may be checked:

1. A local consumer's guide to professional services.
2. Information and referral services, such as a community service organization.
3. An area mental health association.
4. Local clinics, hospitals, or universities.

5. Local (or central) branches of professional organizations.

Although these sources are likely to provide comprehensive information, they generally must maintain an impartial attitude and are therefore not likely to offer a candid evaluation of a particular practitioner or agency. Public reputation is often a clue, but sometimes the popular therapist is the one who pleases rather than effectively intervenes. Some marital and family therapists without academic credentials are very talented. However, in a field where incompetence and fraud are not uncommon, it is safer to choose a therapist who has had reputable training and experience.

Further, since all forms of therapy are a mixture of art and science, the personality of the therapist is also important. Each therapist's concept of therapy is a result of his training, reading, thinking, study, and discussion, his experience as a therapist, the types of people he has worked with, the success he has had, the profession he represents, and most of all, the kind of person he is himself. For example, some therapists—authoritarian in nature—see therapy as a formal doctor–patient relationship where the patient places himself in the doctor's hands for diagnosis and treatment. Others take a decidedly humanistic stance and see it as a relationship between equals—although one is an expert in psychological therapy—designed to facilitate new growth rather than to repair diseased or damaged parts. Those with a more conservative orientation see it as a matter of solving problems, while still others hold to more ambitious goals and view therapy as a process of teaching people to become better problem solvers.

It comes down to this: In making a decision about a therapist, one's own judgment is critical. After credentials, personal qualities, and reputation have been considered, the final decision as to compatibility rests with the couple. The most effective way to make this important decision is to get referrals from several sources, including professional associations, friends, and other professionals, and to shop around. Admittedly, this procedure can be expensive and time-consuming because a few visits to a therapist may be necessary before a reasonable judgment can be made, but it is also possible that the first therapist seen will prove to be quite suitable. To aid in making an informed choice, a list of fifteen questions to be answered after consulting a therapist follows. Responses are scored from 0 to 4; 0=never; 1=slightly or occasionally; 2=sometimes or moderately; 3=a great deal or most of the time; and 4=markedly or all the time. Circle the number that best reflects your feelings and observations and then obtain a total score.

1. The therapist gives me a sense of being understood, of having an ally.     0 1 2 3 4

(Emphathic understanding is important to practically all learning and relearning processes. It is the ingredient of the therapeutic relationship that encourages a person to feel less guarded; when a person feels understood, there is less need to deceive, more inclination to change. There is one caution in evaluating this characteristic: Understanding is not to be equated with agreement. Frequently, the therapist may understand but disagree.)

2. I have a clear idea of the goals I hope to achieve through the therapy process.     0 1 2 3 4

(The process of goal formulation may involve a redefinition of the problem. For example, a couple may begin therapy feeling the main problem is sexual incompatibility. However, it may become apparent that the sexual difficulties are the result of intense hostility between husband and wife. Understanding how they have become so angry with each other may be the initial goal. Often, more than one session is necessary to formulate a mutually agreed upon therapy goal.)

3. The therapist appears alert; he/she does not look bored or distracted.     0 1 2 3 4

(There are many occupations that can be performed adequately by people who are overworked, who are not sensitive to their physical and psychological well-being. Therapy is not among them. If your therapist is consistently tired or distracted, this should be questioned. If the issue is not resolved satisfactorily, look elsewhere for help.)

4. The therapist's suggestions for remedying my difficulties make sense to me.

0  1  2  3  4

(The therapy hour actually represents a very small proportion of an individual's waking time; therefore, in order to facilitate progress, most therapists suggest psychological homework assignments—things to work on during the week. If these suggestions fail to make sense over several sessions, something is wrong. Discuss your confusion; clarification is crucial to continued progress.)

5. The therapist is flexible; he/she is open to new ideas rather than the exclusive pursuit of his/her own point of view.

0  1  2  3  4

(There are many ways to approach a problem; a willingness to consider different methods at different times, according to the demands of the situation, is the mark of a professional. Conversely, rigid adherence to a single approach is a serious limitation.)

6. The therapist is open; he/she will reveal personal issues and feelings when these disclosures are likely to advance the therapy process.

0  1  2  3  4

(The stereotype therapist—an unemotional shadowy figure—does exist, but this type of therapist should be avoided. Effective therapy involves a lively interchange between people. This means that the therapist should be willing to answer questions directly, occasionally reveal personal issues spontaneously, and respond to inquiries about his/her personal life.)

7. The therapist encourages me to confront problems when I attempt to avoid them.   0 1 2 3 4

(A central task of the therapist is to keep the conversation focused on the important—usually uncomfortable—issues that many of us tend to avoid. A therapist who does this effectively may at times seem inconsiderate or harsh. In contrast, if he/she does not do this, you are likely to be dissatisfied with the results of the therapy process.)

8. The therapist is willing to examine his/her own behavior if it is questioned.   0 1 2 3 4

(Frequently, conflicts arise between the therapist and various family members. A competent therapist will not avoid the dispute when it centers directly on him/her. The therapist should also be willing to change; this may include acknowledging being wrong, apologizing for being inconsiderate, and so on. The therapist who, under the guise of professionalism, implies that he/she is always right is to be avoided.)

9. The therapy hour is productive; irrelevant issues and small talk do not characterize the conversation.   0 1 2 3 4

(Change is forged in the fires of struggle; irrelevant, self-serving issues ("Do you have any tips on the stock market?") do not promote this atmosphere. This does not mean that every minute of every session requires sweat and tears to assure progress. Small talk, for example, may provide the bridge that transports the conversation into important problem areas.)

10. The therapist is interested in seeing the significant others in my life—family, relatives, friends—when it seems productive.   0 1 2 3 4

(Psychological functioning is influenced by the way an individual deals with intimate relations, the way they deal with him, and the way other family members involve him in their relations with each other. If your therapist does not want to meet and tune into your relationships with important people in your life, therapy may fail.)

11. The therapist listens and talks in proportions that make sense in the situation.

0  1  2  3  4

(A sensitive therapist will regulate the amount of talk in consideration of the needs of the participants. For example, couples —and their children—are often reluctant to engage one another, particularly initially. The therapist in this instance may be more active while gently encouraging family members to interact with each other. When full participation is under way, the therapist is likely to be much more judicious in his/her intervention.)

12. The therapist appears to have characteristics and qualities to which I aspire; he/she appears to practice what he/she preaches.

0  1  2  3  4

(We can liken the circumstance of individuals seeking marital and family therapy to that of individuals floundering in the water several hundred yards offshore. Perhaps the couple or family does not know how to swim or, knowing how, simply does not have enough strength to make it to shore. The therapist is on shore and has been trained in many life-saving techniques, all of which have been tested in the children's pool. He/she can row a boat; throw out a ring buoy; give artificial respiration. But can he/she swim? The best therapist is one who, given the same circumstance, could swim to shore.)

13. The therapist is open to and encourages differences of opinion rather than

insisting, "You are resisting," each time I disagree with him/her.     0   1   2   3   4

(Whenever we go to a doctor, a lawyer—anybody in authority—the child in us is apt to come out. We don't question; we don't trust our own judgment. A therapist who perpetuates this childlike posture is antitherapeutic.)

14. The therapist treats me as an equal: he/she does not promote the idea that I am defective or unworthy of respect.

                                                    0   1   2   3   4

(An indication that you are with a therapist who treats you as an equal is feeling comfortable with him/her. Further, the therapist without an air of superiority is usually casual and informal rather than stiff and formal.)

15. In general, my contacts with the therapist lead to my feeling more hopeful and to identifiable changes in my life.     0   1   2   3   4

(Many people hesitate to assess changes in themselves because they feel unqualified to judge their own behavior. However, research indicates that in the great majority of instances, an individual undergoing therapy is a good judge of his or her own progress. If after a reasonable period of time—several weeks—there is little or no movement toward a desired goal, bring up your concern in therapy.)

A perfect score *(60 points)* on this instrument is most unlikely. A rating above the mid-40s is an indication of a sound choice; a rating between 30 and 40 is borderline; and a score below 30 is indicative of a poor choice. In marital therapy, it is important that the therapist chosen be rated favorably by both partners because a big difference in this regard is likely to add to an already strain-burdened relationship. As noted previously, it sometimes takes several sessions before a reasonable judgment can be made. Other times, couple-therapist compatibility will be less ambiguous and a much quicker decision will be rendered.

## Cost and Length of Therapy

One of the most important considerations for many couples is the cost of therapy. Professional practitioners' fees vary by region and from one therapist to another. The majority of therapists charge between $25 and $60 per session for their services; a session may last from thirty to sixty minutes. Most private practitioners have a standard fee but some will charge less if a person cannot afford the full fee. Community agencies and family institutes, both public and private, generally have lower fee schedules and may even have a sliding scale based on income. Do not regard size of fee as a reflection of therapeutic skill. There is no relationship. Some competent therapists have a relatively low fee schedule; others bordering on incompetent are exorbitant.

It is customary to be charged for missed appointments when the reason for missing the session is under your control and you fail to give twenty-four to forty-eight hours' advance notice. Group therapy (for individuals, couples, or entire families) is most often of one and a half hour's duration, and is usually billed monthly (fees range from $15 to $35 per appointment) regardless of whether you attend all sessions. This policy is designed to encourage participants to attend all sessions. It is important to learn at the outset the therapist's policy regarding missed appointments, frequency of payment (at each session, monthly, or some other arrangement), and length of sessions. In addition, find out about insurance coverage for therapy. Many health plans provide reimbursement for the services of a qualified psychological professional. None will offer payment for sessions with an unaccredited therapist.

Just as fee schedules and administrative policies of therapists vary, so do recommendations concerning the frequency with which a couple or family needs to see the therapist and the length of time therapy takes. A simple difficulty may be cleared up in a few sessions. A more serious marital or family conflict may require a year or more of therapy. Increasingly, therapists are concentrating on the day-to-day functioning of the family unit rather than making lengthy, detailed excursions into each individual's unconscious motivations and childhood events. Thus, the trend is more and more toward short-term therapy—removing the major obstacle to self-help so that a couple and their children can progress on their own.

Some therapists find it useful to make a "time contract" with a couple. In effect, they all agree upon a certain length of time or a certain number of sessions in which to reach a specific goal. The contract—and goal—may at any time be mutually renegotiated. Whether time-limited therapy is effective or not depends for the most part on how a couple react to it. Some husbands and wives are distressed and distracted by the pressure of an imposed deadline. Others are challenged by it and work more efficiently because there is an end in sight. A couple would be wise to discuss the issue: Do we respond positively to time pressure, or do we resent it? Would we feel more hopeful if we set time limits, or would we feel that we had failed if we did not reach our goal in the scheduled time?

Regardless of the duration of therapy or whether a time schedule is established, it is doubtful that progress will proceed in a neat forward direction. Rather, periods of stagnation, or even backsliding, are to be expected. Freud termed these reverses "negative therapeutic reactions" and ascribed to them an unconscious sense of guilt that barred improvement. While there is good reason to believe that Freud's explanation is ill suited to the dynamics of many people, periods of "two steps back" and stagnation are part of even the most successful therapy experiences.

# Epilogue

As stated at the outset, this book is not a scientific study providing definitive data. The information came from the people interviewed; some came from insights I gained beyond the answers to my questions; information was also obtained from my own life experience and from my clinical practice, as well as from the available research in this area. Statistical studies are a valuable resource, but the experiences and feelings of individuals explored in depth also contribute to our psychological understanding.

Remarriage, as we have seen, is a world of polar opposites, where moments of heightened fulfillment may be followed by moments when happiness appears out of reach. The remarried find themselves inundated by new relationships, awkward stepparenting roles, feelings of bitterness—both aimed at and coming from themselves. These are in addition to shortages of time, money, and energy. Despite these hardships, most members of combined families struggle courageously, and for the most part, successfully. The stereotype of the embattled, unhappy stepfamily—a union of failures—is, in general, nonsense. Nonetheless, there are serious pitfalls in a second marriage and I have at times emphasized these instead of the virtues. Obstacles and problems received the heaviest concentration because to anyone who has lived in a reconstituted family, the joys are self-evident.

The remarried share many of the "normal" problems of primary families, but in addition, they have to contend with unique dilemmas: the attainment of unity by people with separate histories and different concepts of roles; rivalries between stepparent and stepchild and between former mates; and the sometimes severe tension between the married couple as they attempt to make the whole thing work. These are complex problems and do not usually yield to quick resolution. The remarried and their families have generously opened their lives regarding these issues and through this have suggested some guidelines. Here are the highlights:

The dissolution of a marriage whether by divorce or death requires a major psychological repair. This process takes time and will probably begin with a thoroughly disrupted and emotional situation dominated by separation distress, loneliness, and depression, perhaps interrupted by brief intervals of self-confidence and even euphoria. There are likely to be disrupted relationships with others, including, in the case of divorce, an intensely ambivalent relation with the former spouse, uncomfortable contact with relatives, and a dissolution of some friendships and a solidification of others. Financial status will suffer seriously. Frequently, there is much disarray in so many areas that rebuilding a life seems a hopeless task. Yet gradually, after a long process of healing and rehabilitation, coherence and organization return. Most people can expect to love neither judiciously nor fully during this period; in affairs of the heart, wounds are painfully slow to close. Moving into a new marriage immediately diverts the recovery process and is frequently a mistake.

Dating is a necessary element in the healing journey. Most among the formerly married, whatever their ages, begin to date at some point. The possibility of new relationships is the most important reason for dating's attractiveness. But, aside from this, dating allows us to try out our feelings, to exercise them, even if cautiously at first, in order that they may return, in time, to full functioning. Whereas earlier they felt unready for new commitments, most people, after adequate time to heal, are willing to consider a "serious" relationship. This may progress in increments of commitment through going together, a living-together arrangement, and finally, remarriage.

The prognosis for remarriage is essentially positive despite the skepticism of some professionals. Survey studies indicate that men and women appear to be reasonably happy in their second marriages. However, a small proportion of the formerly married may indeed have a very difficult time with a new commitment. Some may be chronically insecure because they have unfinished "emotional business" to contend with. Others may be less willing to accept the obligations of marriage, or they may be prone to fictitious facades—cover-ups for their real feelings—that defeat the possibility of a lasting relationship. Still others are impulsive and reckless in their choice of mate. Even those who enter remarriage after sound consideration are apt to experience difficulty. Second marriages are subject to stresses from which first marriages are relatively free—instant step-relations and ex-spouses.

When one or both of the former mates are filled with animosity, revenge, retaliation, or bitterness, the new marriage is likely to be problematic. When, on the other hand, former husband and wife can treat each other casually and lightly, as people who once had much in common but now lead separate lives, remarriage will probably be accepted by the unmarried ex-spouse and thus stand a better chance of succeeding.

The children involved in a second marriage may not only feel at ease, but even benefit from the widening family circle. This is because children are very adaptable if the environmental conditions are supportive. Frequently the problems with children grow out of unresolved conflicts between the parents. The children may have been used as messengers, weapons, or spies by one parent or the other. In the postmarital period, it is generally warranted and beneficial to bring the children into discussions of such matters as money, parental visits, relationships with grandparents, dating by the parents, new relationships, and lingering resentments over custody decisions. Children, after all, have a stake in these decisions. If they are not included, they can, and often will, sabotage the efforts of their parents to remarry.

The making of a stepchild progresses in three major stages. First, a parent is lost through death or divorce. Next, in consideration of the loss, the child and custodial parent reshape their lives. Finally, the parent remarries requiring the child to make an additional emotional adjustment. As much as parents would like it to occur sooner, the process of a child's adjustment to a new marriage often takes two or three years, sometimes longer. Children must be allowed this time rather than forced to feel things they don't yet (and may never) feel. In addition to the manner in which the loss and interval was handled, the psychological condition of the child previous to any disruption in the home can either magnify or minimize the reaction to remarriage. A child coping with life's difficulties adequately will almost certainly react better to change than the chronically insecure child. For the more psychologically fragile child, professional counseling may be warranted. Early detection and intervention in these instances increases the chance for the child's attaining a reasonable sense of well-being.

Because part of a parent's natural motivation in contemplating remarriage may be to secure a substitute parent for his or her child, there is often an underlying demand for instant love between stepparent and stepchild that can take a burdensome, destructive course. Complicating the issue are the absence of time for marital adjustment before the children come and the ambiguity of the stepparent role. At least three, and often more, individuals have to make a rather abrupt operational adjustment to one another. When only positive feelings are expected (and accepted), all members of the family are in the grip of unnecessary restraints. No other relationship carries such an unrealistic expectation; there is no corollary of this requirement in primary families. In our culture, for example, an adjustment period is understood and condoned when a newborn baby arrives. Yet, we insist on perpetuating the myth of instant love in stepfamilies.

Closer to reality is the fact that even under the best of circumstances the merging of people with different histories and experiences will not progress smoothly; strong feelings will be evoked that need to be aired. This is no simple matter, however, because all members of the family have lived through either abandonment or expulsion—sometimes both—and they are likely to be extremely sensitive to criticism and rejection. They may deal with these feelings through denial (avoidance), destructive acting out, or direct expression. The last option, direct expression, is the healthiest and is promoted when husband and wife respect each other and are open about their feelings. In these instances, conflict is not likely to be damaging—just difficult. Add to this a basic knowledge about parenting, and a willingness to seek outside consultation when necessary, and conflict may turn into an adventure from which all family members can profit.

In remarriages that work well, a common ingredient is that the couple put themselves first; each spouse understands that the relationship takes priority. The couple also understands their obligations toward their children and can meet them more successfully because of their commitment to each other. They are a team and they gear up together to cope; two people with a strong relationship can handle a lot of problems. For their marriage to continue on a firm foundation it is important that each partner: (1) be emotionally aware of the problems that exist and communicate with each other clearly; (2) at the same time put aside the tendency to blame each other; and (3) realize that most problems do not disappear but grow if they are ignored, that a marriage will not prosper by itself.

When the marital relationship is not functioning well and self-help is not effective, professional intervention should be considered. The sooner professional help is sought in these instances, the better. Sometimes therapy including the whole family can be particularly useful. Because the reconstituted family involves two distinct subgroups that have to live together, family treatment, with its emphasis on genuine communication, often enables the fragmented family to achieve a sense of unity. In any case, a careful and informed choice of a competent, compassionate therapist, along with a basic understanding of the therapy process, provides the best chance of successful resolution.

Is there one grand conclusion to be drawn from all this? Hardly. There is, however, a trend to report: The growing concern these days—expressed by leaders in government, by foundations, even by some corporations—to "strengthen the American family" is unjustified. The family as an institution is not in danger of becoming extinct. Practically all of us desire a satisfying, lasting relationship. We have a great capacity—or at least a potential—for intimacy. Yet this is not easy to develop, nor is it always easy to find another person with whom we can have a relationship of mutual growth.

No, the family in America is not dying, it is changing. Longer life spans, greater leisure, and freedom from many of the medical and economic ills that once preoccupied us have encouraged us to raise the level of our emotional aspirations. This is a positive trend that sometimes disrupts a stifling marriage. The result: There is no longer a "typical" American family. Single-parent families, living-together arrangements, communal families, and especially stepfamilies need to be welcomed into the American culture. In times of change, children and adults require support. We can start offering that support by laying to rest the myth of the average American family. In its place we can begin to acknowledge—in our classrooms, in our primary-school readers, in nonfiction works, as well as in our TV shows —the existence, strength, and variety of the families that constitute American society.

# Bibliography

Bergler, Edmund. *Divorce Won't Help.* New York: Harper Brothers, 1948.

Bernard, Jessie. *Remarriage.* New York: The Dryden Press, 1956.

Block, Joel D. *The Other Man, The Other Woman.* New York: Grosset & Dunlap, 1978.

Bohannon, Paul, and Erickson, Rosemary. "Stepping In." *Psychology Today* (January 1978): 53–59.

Duberman, Lucile. *The Reconstituted Family: A Study of Remarried Couples and Their Children.* Chicago: Nelson-Hall Publishers, 1975.

Fisher, Seymour, and Fisher, Rhoda. *What We Really Know about Child Rearing.* New York: Basic Books, Inc., 1976.

Glick, Paul C. "Demographer Looks at American Families." *Journal of Marriage and Family* 37 (February 1975): 15–26.

Hunt, Morton, and Hunt, Bernice. *The Divorce Experience.* New York: McGraw-Hill, 1977.

Locke, Harvey J. *Predicting Adjustment in Marriage.* New York: Henry Holt and Company, 1951.

Maddox, Brenda. *The Half-Parent.* New York: M. Evans and Company, 1975.

Mead, Margaret. "Anomalies in American Postdivorce Relationships," in Paul Bohannon, ed., *Divorce and After.* New York: Anchor Books, 1971.

Messinger, Lillian. "Remarriage Between Divorced People with Children from Previous Marriages: A Proposal for Preparation for Remarriage." *Journal of Marriage and Family Counseling* 2 (April 1976): 193–200.

Simon, Anne W. *Stepchild in the Family.* New York: The Odyssey Press, 1964.

Weiss, Robert S. *Marital Separation.* New York: Basic Books, 1975.

# Acknowledgments

Unfortunately, those to whom I owe the most are the very ones I may not name here; they are the remarried couples and children who permitted me to observe in depth their behavior and communication, and who candidly discussed their fears, discords, and hopes. I am also indebted to the many divorced and widowed people who allowed me entry into their lives during the postmarital period.

Diana Price, my editor, has, again, been quietly and strongly supportive.

Margaret Stumpp was the only typist to whom I would entrust my manuscript.

I am indebted to Gail, Abbey, and Fred Block for providing me with a second-chance family.

# Index

Adverse reactions in remarriage, 35-38
Alimony, 35
American Association of Marriage and Family Counselors (AAMFC), 165, 166
American Board of Psychiatry and Neurology, 161
Attachments, previous, 32-51
Attitudes toward remarriage, 69

Behavior, 24
 in choosing remarriage mates, 67
 interpersonal, 23-27
Bergler, Edmund, 64-65
Bernard, Jesse, 70
Blaming signals in marital relationships, 134-38
 *The Other Man, The Other Woman*, 52-53, 142
Bohannon, Paul, 118-19

Children. *See also* Stepchildren
 as binding agents for parents, 15-16
 "buffering" parental conflicts, 109-10, 112-13
 complicating remarriage, 54
 danger over-spending on, 105
 discipline, 99-101, 107-109
 discontinuation of visits to, by noncustodial parent, 50
 disputes over, 50
 emotional independence, 111
 excuse to provide emotional tie between parents, 33-34
 family roles reshuffled, 81-82
 impact on marriage, 96-113
 involved in second marriage, 177
 jealousy between stepparents and, 102
 in new marriages, 122-24
 noncustodial connection of parents with, 39-42, 50
 parents competing to find fault with, 82-83
 "peacemakers" of parental conflicts, 110
 permanent link to ex-spouses, 71
 pressure on remarriage, 98
 remarriage of parents, 7-9
 role as substitute for missing parent, 80
 role in remarriage of parents, 11

separation anxiety regarding parents, 73
 shielding from truth about parents, 91-92
 as spies, 38
 view of their caretaker, 49
 views may differ from adults', 88
 visits with, 41, 50
 as weapons/buffers, 105-10
Cohabitation, frequency of, 58
Communication
 indirectness and confusion in, 139
 misunderstood, 142
 real two-way, 158
Community reestablishment, 28-29
Comparisons between partners, 45
Conflict of loyalty, 103-105
Contradictions, 44
Contrivances to be avoided, 23-27
Costs, 15-16, 71, 129-30
 new children in new marriages, 123
 therapy, 173-74

Dating (word), 19
Dating between marriages, 18-23, 176-77
Death
 of marriage partner, 176
 of parents, 77, 78
*Directory of Medical Specialists*, 161
Disciplinary practices of parents, 81
 children in remarriages, 99-101, 107-109
 full-time, 49-50
Divorce, 1, 2, 176
 rates, 6
 statistical comparison with remarriage, 72
Divorced
 case histories, 6-9, 15-17, 32-33, 61-63
 psychologically compared with widowed, 14
 reasons for desiring remarriage, 11
Emotions
 deprivation as motive for remarriage, 12
 independence of children in remarriages, 111
 intimacy, 23

**183**

# Index

mourning by widowed, 14
protection need in stepchildren, 122
reaction of stepchildren, 77
realignment of stepchildren, 75
remarriage and, 35
ties of previous attachments, 32-35
wounds, 49
Empathy, 137
Employment, 13-17, 29-30
Entanglements to avoid, case histories of, 42-46
Extramarital romances, 55-57

Family in America, 160
members as separate persons, 158
"reconstituted," 1-2
roles reshuffled in broken, 81-82
therapy. *See* Therapy, marital and family
Feelings, 24
real, 158
weakness, powerlessness, and fear, 48
Financial problems, 15-16, 71, 129-30, 173-74
Fisher, Seymour and Rhoda. *What We Really Know about Child Rearing,* 80
Freudian orientation, 64, 69
Friendliness, 50-51

Glick, Paul, 72
Group therapy, 173

Hunt, Bernice and Morton. *The Divorce Experience,* 72

Impatience, 53
Independence, 56
need for, 145-46
Intimacy and sex in marital relationships, 143-47

Jealousy, 37, 101-103, 107

Living arrangements, 28
Living-together arrangements, 58-63
Locke, Harvey J. *Predicting Adjustment in Marriage,* 70
Love, 98
motive for remarriage, 12
myth in stepfamilies of instant, 179
persistence of former, 32-35
of and from stepchildren, 127-29
Loyalty, conflict of, 103-105

Maddox, Brenda. *The Half-Parent,* 78, 127
Man-woman relationships, 10-11. *See also* Marital relationships; Mates for remarriage; Unmarried
dating between marriages, 18-23
emotional attachment, 16
Marital gripe resolution, 137-38
Marital relationships
arguments frequent and unproductive, 156
avoidance of each other, 157
case histories, 131-32, 135, 140-42, 144-45, 148-49
inflexible, conflicting positions, 156
intimacy and sex in, 143-47
keeping them strong, 131-53
lack of enjoyment and pleasure in company of spouse, 156-57
no sudden collapse, 133
not worth the cost, 155-56
overdependence by one or both partners, 157
quarrelsome couples, 135
questionnaire, 150-53
severe psychological problems or dramatic gestures, 156
sexual dissatisfaction, 157
signals. *See* Signals in marital relationships
work as team to strengthen, 133-34
Marital separation
case histories, 32-35
meaningful activities, 18
recovery, 17, 18
transition, 17-18
Marital therapy. *See* Therapy, marital and family
Marriage and family counselors, 159, 165-66
Marriages. *See also* Remarriages
between, 13-31, 79-84, 92-94
between, and contrivances to avoid, 23-27
broken, 17, 133
dating between, 18-23
dissolution requiring psychological repair, 176
impact of "instant" children on, 96-113
living-together arrangements ending in, 63
Mates for remarriage, 63-69
Mead, Margaret, 119

# Index

Messinger, Lillian, 70-71
Money
 as binding agent for parents, 15-16
 cost of therapy, 173-74
 hassles, 129-30

National Association of Social Workers, 165
*National Register of Health Service Providers in Psychology,* 162, 163
Noncustodial connection of parents with children
 case histories, 39-42
 discontinuation of visits to, 50

Obligation, feeling of in role of custodial parent, 35
Optimism, 5

Parental conflicts
 "buffering" by children, 109-10, 112-13
 children as "peacemakers," 110
 children as weapons/buffers, 105-10
Parenting. *See also* Stepparenting
 divisive dilemmas, 99-105
 how well done in remarriage, 99
 providing emotional tie with former mate, 33-35
Parents. *See also* Stepparents
 competition to find fault with children, 82-83
 death of, 77, 78
 disciplinary practices, 81
 new social activities, 83
 overreacting in discipline when single, 81
 remarriage and children, 84-90, 94-95
Postmarital life, relationships in, 27-31
Powerlessness, feelings of, 48
Psychiatrists, 159-61
Psychological issues, 47-51, 68
Psychologists, 159, 162-63
Psychotherapy, 28, 160

Questions to ask
 choosing marital and family therapist, 168-73
 of marital relationships, 150-53
 self and prospective mate, 68

Reconciliation, 46-51
Rejection, 143
 feeling of, 36

overcompensation cycle in stepparents, 121
Relationships
 guidelines for new, 30-31
 new sibling, 88-90
 in postmarital life, 27-31
Remarriages, 1-3, 5-12, 175
 adverse reactions, 35-38
 case histories, 6-9, 35-58, 53-57, 84-90, 96-98, 100, 102-109
 caution plaguing, 10
 children complicating, 54
 children from earlier marriage and, 84-90, 94-95
 choice of mate, 63-69
 coping process when there are children, 110-13
 facets, 9-12
 issues involving children, 112-13
 keys to success, 179
 mates for. *See* Mates for remarriage
 mistake to provide stepparent for children, 111-12, 178
 new children in, 122-24
 new sibling relationships for children, 88-90
 parenting skills heightened, 112
 parents alert to family, 112
 pressure from children on, 98
 priority marriage, not children, 111
 prognosis, 69-72, 177
 role of children in, 11
 statistical comparison with divorce, 72
 when "someone is waiting," 52-58
Romantic involvement, 32-35, 55-57

Self-disclosure and intimacy, 146
Separation anxiety in children, 73
Separation, marital. *See* Marital separation
Sex and dating between marriages, 20-22
 premeditated ration of intimacies, 21-22
 swingers, 26
Sex and intimacy in marital relationships, 143-47
Sex roles of stepchildren, 75-76
Sibling relationships, 88-90
Signals in marital relationships, 134-50
Simon, Anne. *Stepchild in the Family,* 87
Social workers, 159, 163-65

# Index

Stepchildren
  between marriages of parents, 79-84, 92-94
  case histories, 1, 73-74, 79-80, 82-90
  death of parents, 77, 78
  difficulties in adjusting to stepparents, 119
  disinterested/disliking stepparents, 120-22
  distaste for stepparents, 87
  emotional reaction, 77
  emotional realignment, 75
  implications, 90-95
  loss of natural parent, 73-78, 90-92
  making of, 73-95, 178
  need of emotional protection, 122
  new sibling relationships, 88-90
  pubescence and adolescence, 75
  remarriage of parents, 84-90, 94-95
  sense of betrayal in divorce, 77
  sex roles, 75-76
  uncertain attitudes of parents, 80
Stepparenting, 2, 114-30
  case histories, 115-18, 122-25, 128-29
  confused and mixed feelings about, 130
  myths and realities, 126-30
Stepparents
  difficulties of children in adjusting to, 119
  disciplining of children, 99-101, 107-109
  disinterest or dislike of stepchildren, 120-22
  distaste for by stepchildren, 87
  jealousy between children and, 102
  neglect of many, 114-20
  number, 114
  pressure from selves or mates, 128
  role of stepfather, 117-19
  role of stepmother, 116
  stepmothers compared with stepfathers in public image, 115
  working stepmothers, 124-26
Suicide, thoughts of, 17
Swingers, 26

Therapy, marital and family, 154-74, 179-80
  background and qualifications of therapist types, 159-66
  benefit for children, 158
  considering the need, 154-55
  cost and length of, 173-74
  group therapy, 173
  how to select therapists, 166-73
  one's own judgment in selecting therapist, 167-72
  questionnaire for choosing therapists, 168-73
  real and unreal expectations, 158-59
  recognizing the need, 155-58
Trust and intimacy, 146

Unmarried
  cohabitation, 58
  employment, 29-30
  feeling of not belonging, 11, 28
  living arrangements, 28
  readiness for new relationships, 27-28
  reestablishing community, 28-29
  social activities, 83

Weakness, feelings of, 48
Weiss, Robert S. *Marital Separation,* 17-18, 28
Widowed
  emotional mourning, 14
  psychologically compared with divorced, 14
  reasons for desiring remarriage, 11
Widows between marriages, case histories of, 13-17
Working stepmothers, 13-17